FOUNDATIONS OF BUDDHISM

*"The evolution of the New Era rests on
the cornerstone of Knowledge and Beauty."*

NICHOLAS ROERICH

FOUNDATIONS OF BUDDHISM

BY HELENA ROERICH

AGNI YOGA SOCIETY

2017

Agni Yoga Society
319 West 107th Street
New York NY 10025
www.agniyoga.org

FOREWORD

THE GREAT GOTAMA gave to the world a complete Teaching of the perfect construction of life. Each attempt to make a god of the great revolutionist, leads to absurdity.

Previous to Gotama there was, of course, a whole succession of those who bore the common welfare, but their teachings crumbled to dust in the course of millenniums. Therefore the Teaching of Gotama should be accepted as the first teaching of the laws of matter and the evolution of the world.

Contemporary understanding of the community permits a wondrous bridge from Gotama Buddha up to the present time. We pronounce this formula neither for extolling nor for demeaning, but as an evident and immutable fact.

The law of fearlessness, the law of the renunciation of property, the law of the evaluation of labor, the law of the dignity of human personality, beyond castes and outer distinctions, the law of true knowledge, the law of love based upon self-knowledge, make of the covenants of the Teachers a continuous rainbow of the joy of humanity.

Let us construct the foundations of Buddhism in its manifested covenants. The simple Teaching, equal in beauty to the Cosmos, will dispel every suggestion of idolatry, unworthy of the great Teacher of men.

Knowledge was the leading path of all great Teachers. Knowledge will permit a free and vital approach to the great Teaching, as vitally real as is great Matter itself.

We shall not introduce the latest complexities; we shall speak briefly about those foundations that cannot be denied.

Joy to all peoples! Joy to all those who labor!

The Buddha preaching Dharma. Sarnath, 5th century.

FOUNDATIONS OF BUDDHISM

IN THE FOUNDATIONS of Buddhism, one cannot pause over the later complications and ramifications. It is important to know that the idea of the purification of the Teaching is always alive in the Buddhist consciousness. Soon after the Teacher's death the celebrated councils took place in Rajagriha, and after in Vaishali and Patna, restoring the Teaching to its original simplicity.

The principal existing schools of Buddhism are: the Mahayana (Tibet, Mongolia, the Kalmucks, the Buriats, China, Japan, Northern India) and the Hinayana (Indo-China, Burma, Siam, Ceylon, and India). But both of these schools remember equally well the qualities of the Teacher himself.

The qualities of Buddha are: Muni—the wise, from the clan of Shakya; Shakya Simha—Shakya, the Lion; Bhagavat—the Blessed One; Sadhu—the Teacher; Jina—the Conqueror; the Ruler of the Benevolent Law.

Of unusual beauty is the coming of the King in the image of a mighty mendicant. "Go, ye mendicants, bring salvation and benevolence to the peoples." In this command of Buddha, in this term *mendicants* all is contained.

Understanding the Teaching of Buddha, you realize whence emanates the assertion of the Buddhists— "Buddha is a man." His teaching of Life is above all and every prejudice. The temple does not exist for him, but there is a place of assembly and a home of knowledge—the Tibetan *du-khang* and *tsug-lag-khang*.

Buddha disputed the conventional conception of God. Buddha denied the existence of an eternal and immutable soul. Buddha gave the teaching for every day. Buddha struggled forcefully against possessions. Buddha fought personally against the fanaticism of castes and the privileges of the classes. Buddha affirmed experienced, trustworthy knowledge and the value of labor. Buddha bade the study of the life of the Universe in its full reality. Buddha laid the foundations of the community, foreseeing the victory of the World Community.

Hundreds of millions of worshippers of Buddha are scattered throughout the world and each of them affirms: "I take refuge in the Buddha, I take refuge in the Teaching, I take refuge in the Sangha."

THE BUDDHIST WRITTEN traditions and our contemporary researches have established a series of details of the life of Gotama Buddha. Buddha's death is ascribed by some of the investigators to the year 483 B.C. According to Singhalese chronicles, Buddha lived from 621 to 543 B.C. But Chinese chronicles have fixed the birth of Buddha in the year 1024 B.C. The age of the Teacher at his death is given as about eighty years. The place of the birth of the Teacher is known as Kapilavastu, situated in the Nepalese Terai. The royal line of Shakyas, to which Gotama belonged, is known.

Undoubtedly all biographies of the great Teacher have been greatly elaborated by his contemporaries and followers, especially in the most recent writings, but in order to preserve the coloring and the character of the epoch, we must to a certain extent refer to the traditional exposition.

. . . . .

According to the traditions of the sixth century B.C. the domain of Kapilavastu existed in North India in the foothills of the Himalayas and was populated by numerous tribes of Shakyas, descendants of Ikshvaku of the solar race of Kshatriyas. They were ruled by the Elder of the clan who resided in the city of Kapilavastu, of which no traces are now left; during Buddha's time it was already destroyed by a hostile neighboring king. At that period, Shuddhodana, the last direct descendant of Ikshvaku, reigned at Kapilavastu. Of this king and Queen

Maya was born the future great Teacher, who received the name of Siddhartha, which means—"He who fulfilled his purpose."

Visions and prophecies preceded his birth and the event itself, on the full-moon day of May, was attended with all propitious signs in heaven and on earth. Thus the great Rishi Asita dwelling in the Himalayas, having learned from the Devas that a Bodhisattva, the future Buddha, had been born to the world of men in the Lumbini Park and that he would turn the Wheel of the Doctrine, immediately set out on a journey to pay homage to the future Teacher of men. Reaching the palace of King Shuddhodana, he expressed the desire to see the newborn Bodhisattva. The King ordered the child to be brought to the Rishi, expecting his blessing. But the Rishi on seeing the child, first smiled and then wept. The King anxiously asked the reason of his sorrow and whether he saw an ill omen for his son. To this the Rishi replied that he saw nothing harmful for the child. He rejoiced because the Bodhisattva would achieve full enlightenment and become a great Buddha; and he grieved because his own life was short and he would not live to hear the great Doctrine preached.

Queen Maya, after giving birth to the great Bodhisattva, departed life, and her sister Prajapati took the child and reared it. In Buddhist history she is known as Buddha's first female disciple and the foundress and head of a Sangha for bhikshunis.

. . . . .

On the fifth day, one hundred and eight Brahmins,

versed in the *Vedas*, were invited by King Shuddhodana to his palace. They were to give a name to the newborn Prince and read his destiny by the position of the luminaries. Eight of the most learned said: "He who has such signs as the Prince will become either a Universal Monarch, Cakravartin, or, if he retires from the world, will become a Buddha and remove the veil of ignorance from the sight of the world."

The eighth, the youngest, added, "The Prince will leave the world after seeing four signs: an old man, a sick man, a corpse and an anchorite."

. . . . .

The King, desiring to retain his son and heir, took all measures and precautions to assure this. He surrounded the Prince with all the luxuries and pleasures which his royal power could afford. There are many facts indicating that the Prince Siddhartha received a brilliant education, since knowledge as such was in great esteem in those days, and according to a remark in the *Buddhacarita* by Ashvaghosha, the city of Kapilavastu received its name in honor of the great Kapila—the founder of Sankhya philosophy.

Echoes of this philosophy can be found in the Teaching of the *Blessed One*.

. . . . .

For greater conviction, in the Canon the narrative about his luxurious life at the court of Shuddhodana is put in the words of Buddha himself.

"I was tenderly cared for, bhikshus, supremely so, infinitely so. At my father's palace, lotus pools were built for me, in one place for blue lotus flowers, in one place for white lotus flowers, and in one place for red lotus flowers, blossoming for my sake. And, bhikshus, I used only sandal oil from Benares. Of Benares fabric were my three robes. Day and night a white umbrella was held over me, so that I might not be troubled by cold, heat, dust, chaff, or dew. I dwelt in three palaces, bhikshus; in one, during the cold; in one, in the summer; and in one, during the rainy season. While in the palace of the rainy season, surrounded by musicians, singers, and female dancers, for four months I did not descend from the palace. And, bhikshus, although in the domains of others only a dish of red rice and rice soup would be offered to the servants and slaves, in my father's house not only rice, but a dish with rice and meat was given to the servants and slaves." [1]

But this luxurious and happy life could not appease the great spirit. And in the most ancient traditions we see that the awakening of consciousness to the sufferings and misery of men and to the problems of existence, occurred much earlier than is stated in later writings.

Thus the *Anguttara-Nikaya*, seemingly in Buddha's own words, quotes, "Endowed with such wealth, reared in such delicacy, the thought came—'Verily, the unenlightened worldling, subject himself to old age, without escape from old age, is oppressed when he sees another grown old. I, too, am subject to old age and cannot escape it. If I, who am subject to all this, should see another, who is grown old, oppressed, tormented and sickened, it would not be well with me.' [The same is repeated of sickness and death.] Thus as I reflected on it, all elation in youth utterly disappeared."

. . . . .

From his earliest childhood the Bodhisattva exhibited an unusual compassion and keen mind toward surrounding conditions. According to the *Mahavastu*, the Bodhisattva was taken to the park by the King and his attendants. In this version he was old enough to walk about, and came to a rural village where he saw a serpent and a frog turned up by the plough. The frog was taken away for food and the serpent thrown away. This roused the Bodhisattva to great distress. He was filled with deep sorrow; he felt extreme compassion. Then, desiring complete solitude for his thoughts, he went to a rose-apple tree in an isolated spot; there, seated on the ground, covered with leaves, he fell into thought. His father, not seeing him, became anxious. He was found by one of the courtiers under the shade of the rose-apple tree, deeply engrossed in thought.

. . . . .

Another time he saw the laborers, with hair unkempt, with bare hands and feet, their bodies grimy and bathed with sweat; and the work-oxen goaded with iron prods, their backs and rumps streaming blood, gasping, with fast-beating hearts, burdened by their yokes, bitten by flies and insects, gashed by the ploughshare, with bleeding and festered wounds. His tender heart was touched with compassion.

"To whom do you belong?" he asked the ploughmen.

"We are the King's property," they answered.

"From today you are no longer slaves, you shall no longer be servants. Go wherever you please and live in joy."

He freed the oxen also and said to them, "Go! From today eat the sweetest grass and drink the purest water and may the breezes from the four hemispheres visit you." Then seeing a shady jambu tree, he sat at its foot and gave himself to earnest meditation.

. . . . .

Devadatta seeing a goose flying overhead shot it, and it fell in the garden of the Bodhisattva, who took it and drawing out the arrow, bound up its wound. Devadatta sent a messenger to claim the bird, but the Bodhisattva refused to relinquish it, saying that it belonged not to him who had attempted to take its life, but to him who had saved it.

. . . . .

When the Prince reached his sixteenth birthday, in conformity with the customs of his country he had to choose a consort, after proving himself victor of the Svayamvara contest of arms. The chosen one was the Princess Yashodhara of the same Shakya clan. She became mother of Rahula, who later became his father's disciple and attained Arhatship.

. . . . .

But personal happiness, great as it was, could not satisfy the ardently striving spirit of the Bodhisattva. His heart continued to respond to each human sorrow and his mind, perceiving the transitoriness of all that existed, knew no rest. He roamed through the halls of his palace like a lion stung by some poisoned dart and in pain he groaned, "The world is full of darkness and ignorance; there is no one who knows how to cure the ills of existence!"

This state of his spirit is symbolically described in the four preordained encounters, after which he left his kingdom seeking to deliver the world of its misery. In an ancient biography in verse, following the third encounter, there is the remark that only the Bodhi sattva and his charioteer saw the corpse carried across the road. According to the *Mahapari-Nirvana Sutra* the Prince was then completing his twenty-ninth year.

One day the Prince told Chandaka, his charioteer, that he wanted to drive in the park. While there he saw an old man, and the charioteer explained what old age was and how all were subject to it. Deeply impressed, the Prince turned back and returned home.

A short time after, while out driving, he met a sick man gasping for breath, his body disfigured, convulsed and groaning with pain, and his charioteer told him what disease was and how all men were subject to it. And again he turned back. All pleasures appeared faded to him, and the joys of life became loathsome.

Another time, he came upon a procession with lighted torches bearing a litter with something wrapped in a linen sheet; the women accompanying it had dishevelled hair and were weeping piteously—it was a corpse and Chandaka told him all must come to this state. And the Prince exclaimed: "O worldly men! How fatal is your delusion! Inevitably your body will crumble to dust, yet carelessly, unheedingly, you live on." The charioteer, observing the deep impression these sights had made on the Prince, turned his horses and drove back to the city.

Then another incident happened to the Prince, which seemed to indicate to him the solution of his quest. When they passed by the palaces of the nobility, a Shakya Princess saw the Prince from the balcony of her palace and greeted him with a stanza wherein the word *Nibutta* (Nirvana) recurred in each line, which means:

> "Happy the father that begot you,
> "Happy the mother that nursed you,
> "Happy the wife that calls husband
> "This, Lord so glorious.
> "She has gone beyond sorrow."

The Prince, hearing the word *Nibutta*, loosened from his neck a precious pearl necklace and sent it to the princess as a reward for the instruction she had given him. He thought:

"Happy are they that have found deliverance. Longing for peace of mind I shall seek the bliss of Nirvana."

On the same night Yashodhara dreamt that the Prince was abandoning her and she awoke and told him of her dream. "O, my Lord, wherever thou goest, there let me also go."

And he, thinking of going where there was no sorrow (Nirvana), replied, "So be it, wherever I go, there mayest thou go also."

After Buddha's return, Yasodhara, together with his foster mother Prajapati, became his first female disciples.

. . . . .

It was night. The Prince could not find peace on his couch. He arose and went forth into the garden. He sat down beneath the great jambu tree and gave himself to thought, pondering on life, on death, and the evils of decay. He concentrated his mind, became free from confusion, and perfect tranquillity came over him. In this state his mental eye opened and he beheld a lofty figure endowed with majesty, calm and dignified. "Whence comest thou and who mayest thou be?" asked the Prince. In reply the vision said: "I am a Shramana. Troubled at the thought of old age, disease, and death, I have left my home to seek the path of salvation. All things hasten to decay; only the truth abideth forever. Everything changes, and there is no permanency; yet the words of the Buddhas are immutable."

Siddhartha asked: "Can peace be gained in this world of sorrow? I am overcome with the emptiness of pleasure and have become disgusted with lust. All oppresses me, and existence itself seems intolerable."

The Shramana replied: "Where heat is, there is also a possibility of cold. Creatures subject to pain possess the faculty of pleasure. The origin of evil indicates that good can be developed. For these things are correlatives.

Thus where there is much suffering, there will be much bliss, if thou but open thine eyes to behold it. Just as a man who has fallen into a heap of filth should seek the nearby pond covered with lotuses, just so seek thou the great deathless lake of Nirvana to cleanse the defilement of sin. If the lake is not sought, it is not the fault of the lake, just so, when there is a blessed road leading the man bound by sin to the salvation of Nirvana, it is not the fault of the road, but of the man, if the road be not trod. And when a man burdened with sickness does not avail himself of the help of a physician who can heal him, it is not the fault of the physician; so, when a man oppressed by the malady of wrong-doing does not seek the spiritual guide of enlightenment, it is not the fault of the sin-destroying guide."

The Prince listened to the wise words and said: "I know that my purpose will be accomplished but my father tells me that I am still too young, that my pulse beats too full to lead a Shramana's life."

The venerable figure replied: "Thou shouldst know that for seeking truth no time can be inopportune."

A thrill of joy pierced Siddhartha's heart. "Now is the time to seek the truth. Now is the time to sever all ties that would prevent me from attaining perfect enlightenment."

The celestial messenger heard the resolution of Siddhartha with approval: "Go forth, Siddhartha, and fulfill thy purpose. For thou art Bodhisattva, the Buddha-elect; thou are destined to enlighten the world. Thou art the Tathagata, the Perfect One, for thou shall fulfill all righteousness and be Dharma-raja, the King of Truth. Thou art Bhagavat, the Blessed One, for thou art summoned to become the saviour and redeemer of the world.

"Do thou fulfill the perfection of Truth. Though the thunderbolt descend upon thy head, never yield to the allurements that beguile men from the path of truth. As the sun at all seasons pursues its own course nor seeks another, just so if thou forsake not the straight path of righteousness, thou shall become a Buddha.

"Persevere in thy quest and thou shall find what thou seekest. Pursue thy aim unswervingly and thou shall conquer. The benediction of all deities, of all that seek light is upon thee, and heavenly wisdom guides thy steps. Thou shall be the Buddha, thou shall enlighten the world and save mankind from perdition."

Having thus spoken, the vision vanished, and Siddhartha's soul was filled with ecstacy. He said to himself: "I have awakened to the Truth and I am resolved to accomplish my purpose. I will sever all ties that bind me to the world, and I will go out from my home to seek the way of salvation. Verily, I shall become a Buddha."[3]

The Prince returned to the palace for a last glance of farewell upon those whom he loved above all treasures of Earth. He went to the abode of the mother of Rahula and opened the door of Yashodhara's chamber. There burnt a lamp of scented oil. On the bed, strewn with jasmine, slept Yashodhara, the mother of Rahula, with her hand on the head of her son. Standing with his foot at the threshold, the Bodhisattva looked at them and his heart grieved. The pain of parting smote him. But nothing could shake his resolution and with a courageous heart he suppressed his feelings and tore himself away. He mounted his steed Kanthaka, and finding the castle gates wide open he passed out into the silent night accompanied only by Chandaka his faithful charioteer. Thus Siddhartha, the Prince, renounced worldly pleasures, gave up his kingdom, severed all ties, and went into homelessness. [2]

U P TO NOW, four sites in India have drawn the pilgrimages of devotees to the Teaching of the Blessed Buddha. His birthplace, Kapilavastu, was a city situated in the north of India, on the foothills of the Himalayas, at the source of the river Gandak, and was destroyed even during the life of Buddha. The place of his enlightenment, Buddhagaya, where was Uruvela, the often-mentioned grove, under the shade of which Gotama united all his attainments in illumination. The place of his first sermon, Sarnath (near Benares), where, according to the legend, Buddha set in motion the Wheel of the Law, still shows traces of ruins of most ancient communities. The place of his death—Kushinara (Nepal).

In the notes of the Chinese traveler Fa-Hsien (A.D. 392–414), who visited India, we find a description of the domain of Kapilavastu as well as of other revered spots.

Despite these facts, despite the ancient columns of King Ashoka, there are those who love to make of the Buddha a myth, and to separate this high Teaching from life. The French writer Senart, in a special work, affirms that Buddha was a solar myth. But here, also, science has restored the human personality of the Teacher, Gotama Buddha. The urn with part of the ashes and bones of Buddha, found in Piprawa (Nepalese Terai) bearing a date and inscription, as well as an historical urn with some relics of the Teacher, buried by King Kanishka and found near Peshawar, bear definite testimony

23

to the death of the first Teacher of the World Community, Gotama Buddha.

One should not think that the life of Gotama Buddha was spent in universal acknowledgment and quiet. On the contrary, there are indications of slander and all kinds of obstacles, through which the Teacher, as a true fighter, only strengthened himself, thus augmenting the significance of his achievement. Many incidents speak about the hostility which he encountered from ascetics and Brahmins, who hated him. The former for his reproval of their fanaticism, the latter for his refusal to admit their rights to social privileges and to the knowledge of truth by right of birth.

To the first, he said: "If only through the renunciation of food and human conditions one could attain perfection and liberation from the bonds which tie man to Earth, then a horse or a cow would have reached it long ago."

To the second: "According to his deeds a man becomes a pariah; according to his deeds he becomes a Brahmin. The fire kindled by a Brahmin, and the fire kindled by a Shudra have an equal flame, brightness, and light. To what has your isolation brought you? In order to procure bread you go to the general market, and you value the coins from the purse of a Shudra. Your isolation may be termed merely plunder. And your sacred implements are merely instruments of deception.

"Are not the possessions of the rich Brahmin a desecration of the Divine Law? You consider the south as light and the north as darkness. A time will come when I shall come from the midnight and your light shall be extinguished. Even the birds fly north to bear their young. Even the gray geese know the value of earthly possession. But the Brahmin tries to fill his girdle with gold and to hoard his treasures under the threshold of his house. Brahmin, you lead a contemptible life and your end shall be pitiable. You shall be the first to be visited with destruction. If I go northward, then shall I also return from there." (Taken from oral traditions of Buddhists in India.)

There are established cases when, after his discourses, a great many of the listeners deserted him and the Blessed One said: "The seed has separated from the husk; the remaining community, strong in conviction, is established. It is well that the conceited ones have departed."

Let us remember the episode when his nearest disciple and relative, Devadatta, conceived the thought of throwing a stone at the passing Teacher and even succeeded in injuring his toe. [29]

Let us remember the cruel destiny which visited his clan and country through the vengeance of the neighboring king. The legends relate that Buddha, being far from the city with his beloved disciple Ananda at the time of the attack on his country, felt a severe headache and lay down on the ground, covering himself with his robe, in order to hide from the only witness the sorrow which overcame his stoical heart.

Neither was he exempt from physical ailments. Severe pains in his back are often mentioned and even his death was the result of poisonous food. All these details make his image verily human and close to us.

THE WORD *BUDDHA* is not a name, but indicates the state of a mind which has reached the highest point of development; literally translated, it means the "enlightened one," or the one who possesses perfect knowledge and wisdom.

According to the Pali Suttas, Buddha never claimed the omniscience which was attributed to him by his disciples and followers: "Those who told thee, Vaccha, that the Teacher Gotama knows all, sees all, and asserts his possession of limitless powers of foresight and knowledge and says, 'In motion or immobility, in vigilance or sleep, always and in all, omniscience dwells in me,' those people do not say what I said, they accuse me despite all truth." [4]

The powers possessed by Buddha are not miraculous, because a miracle is a violation of the laws of nature. The supreme power of Buddha coordinates completely with the eternal order of things. His superhuman abilities are miraculous, inasmuch as the activities of a man must appear miraculous to the lower beings. To self-sacrificing heroes, to fighters for true knowledge, it is as natural to manifest their unusual achievements as for a bird to fly or for a fish to swim.

Buddha, according to one text, "is only the elder of men, differing from them no more than as the hatched chick differs from later chicks of the same hen." Knowledge uplifted him to a different order of beings, because the principle of differentiation lies in the depth of consciousness.

The humanness of Gotama Buddha is especially underlined in the most ancient writings, where the following expression is met, "Gotama Buddha, the most perfect of bipeds."

The Pali Suttas contain many vivid definitions of the high qualities of Gotama, the Teacher, who indicated the path. Let us mention some of them: "He is the leader of the caravan, the founder, the teacher, the incomparable trainer of men." [1] "Humanity was rolling like a cartwheel on the way to its destruction, lost without guide and protector. He indicated to it the right path. He is the Lord of the Wheel of Benevolent Law. He is the Lion of the Law." [5]

"He is a wondrous physician; by compassionate means he cures dangerously sick people." [6]

"The venerable Gotama is a ploughman. His field is immortality." [7]

"He is the light of the world. He it is who lifts one from Earth. He it is who unveils that which is concealed. He it is who carries the torch in the darkness, in order that those who have eyes may see; thus Gotama illumined his Teaching from all sides."

"He is the Liberator. He liberates, because he himself has been liberated." His moral and spiritual perfection testifies to the Truth of his Teaching, and the power of his influence upon those who surrounded him rested on the example of his personal labor.

Ancient writings always emphasize the vital applicability of his teaching. Gotama did not avoid life, but took part in the daily life of the workers. He tried to direct them toward the Teaching, offered them participation in his communities, accepted their invitations and did not fear to visit courtesans and rajas, the two centers of social life in the cities of India. He tried not to offend unnecessarily the traditional customs; furthermore he sought the possibility of giving them his Teaching, finding support for it in an especially revered tradition not conflicting with the basic principles.

There was no abstraction in his Teaching. He never opposed the ideal of mystic and transcendental life to existing reality. He stressed the reality of all existing things and conditions for the current moment. And as his activities and thoughts were concerned mostly with the circumstances of life, he drew the contents of his speeches and parables out of daily life, using the simplest images and comparisons.

Starting from the concept of the parallel between nature and human life, Hindu thinkers believe that the manifestations of nature can explain many things to us in the manifestations of life. Using this method, Buddha, fortunately for his Doctrine, retained the experience of this old tradition. "I shall show thee by comparison, because many rational people understand by comparison"—such was the usual formula of Buddha. And this simple, vital approach lent to his Teaching vividness and conviction.

His influence upon people was proportionate to his faith in himself, in his power, and in his mission.

He always adapted himself to the situation of each pupil and listener, giving to them the most needed, in accordance with their understanding. He did not burden the disciples and listeners, who were unprepared to absorb the highest knowledge, with intricate intellectual processes. Nor did he encourage those who sought abstract knowledge, without applying in life his highly ethical Teaching. Once, when one such questioner, named Malunkya, asked the Blessed One about the origin of all things, the Blessed One remained silent, because he considered the most important task lay in affirmation of the reality of our surroundings; this meant to see things as they exist around us, and try first to perfect them, to prompt their evolution and not to waste time on intellectual speculation.

Certainly his knowledge was not limited to his Doctrine, but caution prompted by great wisdom made him hesitant to divulge conceptions which, if misunderstood, might be disastrous.

Once the Blessed One was staying at Kausambi in the Simsapa Grove. And the Blessed One, taking a few simsapa leaves in his hand, said to his disciples, "What think you, my disciples, which are more, these few leaves I hold in my hand, or the remaining leaves in the Simsapa Grove above?

"The leaves that the Blessed One holds in his hand are few in number; far more are the leaves in the Simsapa Grove above.

"Just so, disciples, what I have perceived and not communicated to you is far more than what I have communicated to you. And why, O disciples, have I not revealed this to you? Because it would be of no advantage to you, because it does not contribute to the higher life, because it does not lead to disgust with the world, to annihilation of all lust, to the ceasing of the transitory, to peace, to higher knowledge, to awakening, to Nirvana. Therefore I have not communicated it to you. And what have I communicated to you? That which is suffering, the source of suffering, the cessation of suffering and the path that leads to the cessation of suffering." [14]

And so individual and practical was his Teaching in each separate case, that the tradition of three circles of the Teaching was established: for the chosen ones, for the members of the Sangha, and for all.

In founding his Sanghas, Buddha strove to create the best conditions for those who had firmly determined to work upon the expansion of their consciousness for the attainment of higher knowledge. Then he sent them into life as teachers of life, as heralds of a World Community.

The constant discipline of words, thoughts, and deeds demanded of his disciples, without which there can be no success on the way to perfection, is almost unattainable for those in the midst of the usual conditions of life, where a thousand outer circumstances and petty obligations constantly divert the striving one from his aim. But life among people united by the same aspiration, by common thoughts and habits, was a great aid, because without loss of energy it provided possibilities to develop in the desired direction.

Buddha—who taught that in the whole Universe only

correlatives exist; who knew that *nothing exists without cooperation*; who understood that the selfish and conceited one could not build the future because, by the cosmic law, he would be outside the current of life which carries all that exists toward perfection—patiently planted the seeds, establishing the cells on a community basis, foreseeing in the distant future the realization of the great World Community.

. . . . .

Two rules were necessary for admission into the community: complete renunciation of personal possession, and moral purity. The other rules were concerned with severe self-discipline and obligations to the community. Each one entering the community pronounced the formula: " 'I take refuge in the Buddha, I take refuge in the Teaching, I take refuge in the Sangha,' as the destroyers of my fear." The first with his Teachings, the second by its immutable truth, and the third by its example of the great law expounded by Buddha.

The renunciation of property was austerely carried into life. Besides, the renunciation of property had to be shown not so much externally as accepted in consciousness.

Once a pupil asked the Blessed One, "How should one understand the fulfillment of the Covenant regarding the renunciation of property? One disciple renounced all things but his Teacher continued to reproach him for possession. Another remained surrounded by objects but did not merit reproach."

"The feeling of possession is measured not by objects but by thoughts. One may have objects and still not be a possessor."

Buddha always advised the possession of as few objects as possible in order not to devote too much time to them.

The entire life of the community was strictly disciplined, for the foundation of Buddha's Teaching was iron self-discipline, in order to bridle uncontrolled feelings and thoughts and to develop indomitable will. Only when the disciple mastered his senses did the Teacher slightly raise the veil and assign a task. Only thereafter was the pupil gradually admitted to the depth of knowledge. Out of such men, disciplined and trained by austere renunciation of everything personal and consequently virile and fearless, did Gotama Buddha desire to create workers for the common welfare, creators of the people's consciousness and forerunners of the World Community.

Valor was cemented into the foundation of all achievements in the Teaching of Gotama. "There is no true compassion without valor; no self-discipline can be achieved without valor; patience is valor; one cannot fathom the depth of true knowledge and acquire the wisdom of an Arhat without valor." Gotama demanded from his disciples complete annihilation of any sense of fear. Fearlessness of thought, fearlessness of action were ordained. The very appellation of Gotama Buddha, "Lion," and his personal summons to walk through all obstacles like a rhinoceros or elephant, shows what depths of fearlessness he ordained. Hence,

the Teaching of Gotama may be called first of all the
Teaching of Fearlessness.

> "Warriors we call ourselves, O disciples,
>> because we wage war.
> "We wage war for lofty virtue, for high endeavor,
>> for sublime wisdom.
> "Therefore we are called warriors." [1]

ACCORDING TO TRADITION, the attainment of illumination by Gotama was marked by the revelation of "the chains of causation" (Twelve Nidanas). The problem which tormented him for many years was solved. Meditating from cause to effect, Gotama revealed the source of evil:

12) Existence is pain, because it contains old age, death and myriads of pains.
11) I suffer because I am born.
10) I am born because I belong to the world of existence.
9) I exist because I nourish existence within me.
8) I nurture existence because I have desires.
7) I have desires because I have sensations.
6) I have sensations because I come in touch with the outer world.
5) This touch is produced by the action of my six senses.
4) My senses are manifested because being a personality I oppose myself to the impersonal.
3) I am a personality because I have a consciousness imbued with the consciousness of this personality.
2) This consciousness was created as a consequence of my former existences.
1) These existences obscured my consciousness because I had no knowledge.

It is customary to enumerate this twelvefold formula in the reverse order:

1. *Avidya* (obscuration, ignorance).
2. *Samskara* (karma).
3. *Vijnana* (consciousness).
4. *Nama-rupa* (form—the sensuous and nonsensuous).
5. *Shad-ayatana* (the six transcendental bases of feelings, sensations).
6. *Sparsha* (the touch).
7. *Vedana* (feelings).
8. *Trishna* (thirst, craving).
9. *Upadana* (strivings, attachments).
10. *Bhava* (existence).
11. *Jati* (birth).
12. *Jara* (old age, death).

Thus, the source and the primary cause of all human sufferings lie in obscurity and ignorance. From this issue Gotama's definitions and condemnations precisely of ignorance. He affirmed that ignorance is the greatest crime because it is the cause of all human sufferings, compelling us to value that which is unworthy of being valued; to suffer where there should be no suffering; to take the illusion for the reality; to spend one's life pursuing the insignificant, neglecting what in reality is the most precious: knowledge of the mystery of human existence and destiny.

The light which could dispel this darkness and give liberation from suffering was proclaimed by Gotama Buddha as the knowledge of the Four Noble Truths:

1) The pain of embodied existence, caused by constantly recurring births and deaths.

2) The cause of these sufferings lies in ignorance, in the thirst for self-gratification through earthly possessions which drag after them the perpetual repetition of imperfect existence.

3) The cessation of sufferings lies in the attainment of a state of enlightened all-inclusiveness, thus creating the possibility of conscious interception of the circle of earthly existence.

4) The path to cessation of these pains consists in gradual strengthening of the elements necessary to be perfected for the annihilation of the causes of earthly existence and for approaching the great truth.

The path to this truth was divided by Gotama into eight parts:

1. Right understanding (that which concerns the law of causes).
2. Right thinking.
3. Right speech.
4. Right action.
5. Right living.
6. Right labor.
7. Right vigilance and self-discipline.
8. Right concentration.

A man who has applied these points to life is freed from the pain of earthly existence which is the consequence of ignorance, desire, and longings. When this liberation is achieved, Nirvana is attained.

What is Nirvana? "Nirvana is the capacity to contain all actions, it is the limit of all-inclusiveness. The tremor of illumination attracts true knowledge. Quiescence is only an outer sign, not expressing the essence of this state." According to our contemporary understanding we may define Nirvana as a state of perfection of all the elements and energies in an individual, brought to the limit of intensity attainable in the present cosmic cycle.

Gotama Buddha also pointed out ten great obstacles, called fetters:

1. The illusion of personality.
2. Doubt.
3. Superstition.
4. Physical passions.
5. Hatred.
6. Attachment to Earth.
7. Desire for enjoyment and rest.
8. Pride.
9. Self-contentment.
10. Ignorance.

To reach the higher knowledge it is necessary to shake off these fetters.

In Buddhism are expounded to the minutest details the subdivisions of the senses and the motives of the intellectual process as obstacles to or means of development for the facilitation of self-knowledge, through mental training and analyzing each object in detail. Following this method of self-knowledge man ultimately reaches the knowledge of true reality, sees truth as it is. This is the method applied by each wise teacher for the development of the disciple's mind.

Preaching the Four Noble Truths and the noble path, Gotama condemned, on one hand, the bodily mortifica-

tion practised by ascetics, and, on the other, licentious-
ness—indicating the path of the eight steps as the way
of the harmonization of the senses and the attainment
of the six perfections of an Arhat: compassion, morality,
patience, valor, concentration, and wisdom.

Buddha insisted upon the realization by his disciples
of the concept of two extremes, since the perception
of Reality is achieved only through the juxtaposition
of two extremes. If the disciple was unable to master
this, the Blessed One did not introduce him to further
knowledge, for it would be not only useless but even
harmful. The realization of this concept was facilitated
by the assimilation of the principle of relativity. Buddha
affirmed the relativity of all that exists, pointing out the
eternal changes in nature and the impermanency of all
things in the stream of boundless existence eternally
striving toward perfection. And the extent to which he
adhered to this principle of relativity may be seen from
the following parable:

"Suppose," said the Buddha to his followers one day,
"suppose that a man setting out upon a long journey is
confronted by a great body of water, the nearer side of
which is beset with many perils and dangers, but the
farther side, secure and free of danger; that there is no
boat wherewith to cross the flood, nor any bridge leading
to the other shore. And suppose this man should say to
himself, 'Truly, this is a great and wide body of water, but
of means wherewith to get to the other shore there are
none. Suppose I gather reeds and branches and leaves
and from them make a raft for myself, and supported

on my raft and paddling with hands and feet cross to the safety of the other shore!' Then suppose this man does as he has said and makes a raft, launches it upon the water and, working hands and feet, arrives safely on the other shore.

"And now, after crossing and upon reaching the opposite shore, suppose the man should say, 'Verily, this raft has been serviceable to me, for by means of it, working hands and feet, I have safely crossed to this other shore. Suppose I lift up my raft and put it on my head or shoulders and so proceed upon my way!'

"What think ye, disciples? By so doing, would the man be acting rightly regarding his raft?

"What, then, should such a man do to act rightly regarding his raft?

"Then, disciples, this man ought to say to himself, 'Truly, this raft has been very serviceable to me, for supported by this raft and working hands and feet, I have crossed safely to this farther shore. But suppose I lay it on the bank and proceed with my journey!' Thus, this man would be acting rightly in the matter of his raft.

"In the same manner also, disciples, do I put my Teaching before you in the analogy of a raft, designed as a means of escape, not a constant possession. Understand clearly this analogy of a raft: Dharma is to be left behind when you cross to the shore of Nirvana." [4]

Here we see what little importance is to be attached to anything in this world of relativity—Maya. Everything, even the Teaching of a Perfectly Enlightened One, is of merely provisory, transitory, relative value. This parable also stresses the necessity of exertion through human hands and feet, the Teaching being effective only if personal efforts are applied to it.

. . . . .

Buddha's communities gave shelter to the most varied demands and therefore were gathered out of the most varied elements. In the *Milinda Panha*, we find the following: "What causes impel one to join the community?" Milinda once asked his Buddhist teacher Nagasena. The sage answered that some become adherents of the Sangha in order to escape the tyranny of a ruler; others join to save themselves from brigands or are overburdened with debts, but there are also some who simply wish to have their existence provided for.

If some joined the community in search of social and material privileges, more numerous were the true social reformers, gathered under the broad shelter of possibilities, which the Teaching of Buddha offered in the midst of the dark feudal reality of his era. In the *Sutta Nipata* one finds severe condemnations of the social stamina and public morality of that era.

The community admitted all without distinction of race, caste, or sex, and the most varying quests and searchings of new ways found satisfaction in it.

Buddha's communities were not monasteries, and admission to them was not an initiation. According to the words of the Teacher, the realization of the Teaching alone made of the neophyte a new man and a member of the community.

Full equality of all members existed in the community. One member differed from another, by the date of his admission. At the election of the Elder age was not taken into consideration. Seniority was not measured by gray hair. About one whose merit rested only on his old age, it was said that he was "old-in-vain." But "he is an Elder in whom justice speaks, who knows how to master himself, who is wise."[8]

Buddha did not demand living in a closed community. From the very beginning, among the disciples there were some who preferred the solitary life. About those who isolated themselves too greatly, Buddha said: "A solitary life in the forest is useful to him who pursues it, but of little help to the welfare of men."

Buddha did not wish to establish too many rules. He strove to avoid pedantry and uniformity of regulations, as well as the imposition of too many prohibitions. All rules were directed toward protecting and safeguarding the complete independence of the disciple. The member of the community was obliged to observe simplicity and decency, but as there lie no spiritual preferences in how to be nourished and how to dress, Buddha left a certain freedom to the disciples. Incited by Devadatta, some of the disciples asked Buddha to establish a more strict discipline for the community and to forbid the use of meat and fish. Buddha refused their request, saying that each one was free to apply to himself these measures but they should not be imposed as an obligation for all. The same tolerance was permitted in attire, as it was inadmissible that freedom should degenerate into a privilege for the few. Confident of the wisdom of the venerable Sona, the Blessed One said to him: "Sona, thou hast been raised in refinement, I command thee to wear shoes with soles." Sona then asked that this permission be extended to all members of the Sangha and the Blessed One quickly acceded to this request. [9]

In the *Vinaya* we see how all regulations in the community established by the Blessed One were always instigated by a vital necessity. In the *Vinaya* text II, page 240, a touching episode which resulted in a new rule for the Sangha is cited.

One time a certain bhikshu had an illness of the bowels and he lay fallen in his own excrement. Now when the Blessed One, followed by the venerable Ananda, passed through the sleeping quarters, he came to the cell of the bhikshu and saw him in this condition.

And seeing, he went to him and said,

"What is it, bhikshu, are you ill?"

"I have an illness of the bowels, Lord."

"Have you no one to tend you, bhikshu?"

"No, Lord."

"Why do not the bhikshus tend you?"

"Because, Lord, I am of no service to the bhikshus."

Whereupon the Blessed One said to the venerable Ananda, "Go, Ananda, and bring water, let us bathe this bhikshu."

"Yes, Lord," replied the venerable Ananda to the Blessed One, and brought the water. Then the Blessed One poured the water while the venerable Ananda washed him. And the Blessed One holding him by the head, and the venerable Ananda by the feet, they lifted him and laid him upon his bed.

Then on that occasion and in that connection, the Blessed One called a meeting of the Order and asked the bhikshus, "Bhikshus, in such-and-such a quarter is there a bhikshu who is sick?"

"Yes, Lord."

"And, bhikshus, what is the matter with him?"

"He has an illness of the bowels, Lord."

"And is there anyone to tend him, bhikshus?"

"No, Lord."

"But why do not the bhikshus tend him? Bhikshus, you have neither mothers nor fathers who may wait upon you. If, bhikshus, you do not wait upon one another, who, forsooth, will tend you? Whoever, bhikshus, would wait upon me should tend the sick.

"If he have a preceptor, his preceptor should wait upon him until he is recovered and the same if he have a teacher, a co-disciple of the same Vihara, or a disciple lodging with his teacher. And if he have none of these, then the Sangha should tend him; and whoever does not do so, shall be guilty of offense." [9]

The Teacher's dislike to establish numerous and static rules, especially forbiddances, and the desire to safeguard the vitality of the communal life are vividly expressed in his last covenants to his disciple Ananda, "I entrust the community to alter the small and minutest rules." [19]

But many weak souls are more at ease if their obligations are strictly defined; hence originated the multiplicity of rules and forbiddances of later Buddhism. It is much easier to submit to rules, even under constraint, than to manifest the personal conscious energy which the Teacher demanded of his disciples. The community strove not to deprive the members of their personalities, but to unite them in friendship and closeness in a single aspiration toward general well-being. The community did not desire to level individual peculiarities; on the contrary, Buddha appreciated each evidence of initiative, each individual manifestation, because the Teaching asserts that each one is his own creator and liberator, and that personal efforts are absolutely necessary to achieve this high goal. Thus the individual origin had all possibilities for development. "Avoid quarrels, being affirmed in one's own self, not excluding others." This was accepted as a rule in the community.

And so little did Buddhism fear individual manifestations, that often the inspired words of one of the members of the community were accepted and became part of the Canon together with the covenants of the Teacher.

Severe discipline, constant watch over thought, word, and deed, made out of the community a school, as much a training one as educational. The Teacher, who pronounced knowledge the one means of escape from earthly fetters, and ignorance, the most heinous crime, ordained all to walk the path of knowledge.

Parallel with the condemnation of ignorance we find an equally stern condemnation of frivolity.

"The fools, the ignorant, are their own greatest enemies, for they do evil deeds which bear bitter fruits.

"Though a fool be companion to a wise man his whole life long, he yet remains ignorant of the Truth, as does the spoon of the savor of the soup.

"Long is the night to the watcher, long is the mile to the weary. Long is the round of lives and deaths to fools that know not the Truth."[8]

He especially made a point of often telling parents to teach their children all sciences and arts and thereby help the growth of their consciousness. He likewise constantly pointed out the vital necessity of travel. Therein he saw a really instructive purpose, for travel tearing man away from daily circumstances, develops in him mobility, resourcefulness, and adaptability—indispensable qualities preparatory to the process of expansion of consciousness.

The Teaching of Gotama demands authenticity, but it has no dogmas which are to be taken on good faith, because the Teacher, affirming knowledge in all things, saw no use in blind faith for the development of consciousness. "Therefore," said Buddha, "I have taught you to believe not because you have heard, but only when your consciousness has verified and accepted."

In a talk with a young Brahmin, Buddha pointed out how a worthy disciple attains a mastery of the Truth: "When, after a mature consideration, the disciple acknowledges that the indicated man is entirely free from possibility of error, he trusts this man. Approaching him with trust, he becomes his disciple. Having become his disciple, he opens his ear. Having opened his ear, he harkens to the Teaching. Having heard the Teaching, he retains it in his mind. He analyzes the meaning of the truths that he has retained. He meditates upon it. From this is born his decisiveness. What he has decided he will undertake. He appreciates the significance of the undertaken. Having appreciated, he applies all efforts. By applied efforts he approaches the Truth. Having penetrated into its depths, he sees. Yet all this is only the recognition of the Truth, not its possession. In order to master it completely, one has to apply, to nurture, and to untiringly repeat this psychological process." [4]

From this discourse it is clear how free the disciple was to discuss the Teaching given to him, and that knowledge and mastery of the truth are attained only by self-exertion.

．　．　．　．　．

The Teaching of Buddha, as a Teaching of Truth, embraced all the preceding great teachings and therefore, stressing their truth, it rejected denial. Rejecting denial the Teaching did not subordinate anyone. The realization of the great principle of cooperation opened all ways.

In Buddha's communities, a personally realized renunciation was permitted, but a denial was compared to ignorance. In the communities of Buddha one could renounce petty considerations, but a denial was equal to a withdrawal from the community. It was customary never to mention the one who left—the community had to live for the future. Besides, the departed one often returned; then the return was never followed by any questions except one: "Dost thou no longer deny?"

At the beginning of the Teaching, the discipline chiefly concerned the purification of the heart and mind of all prejudices and bad qualities. According to the progress, the emphasis of the Teaching was transferred and concentrated upon the expansion of consciousness.

It is difficult for a man to rise without passing through the severe trial of purification. "If the cloth be dirty, however much the dyer might dip it into blue, yellow, red, or lilac dye, its color will be ugly and unclear—why? Because of the dirt in the cloth. If the heart is impure one must expect the same sad result."[4]

"I say that it is not sufficient to wear a robe, to be a striving one. It is not enough to be naked, covered with mud, sprinkled with water, to sit beneath a tree, to live in solitude, to stand in one position, to starve oneself, to repeat mantras and to twist one's hair."[4] "A man is not a mendicant simply because he is being fed through alms."[8] "A man is not an ascetic only because he lives in a forest."[5] " Unworthy of the yellow garment is he who wears it and is impure and insincere in deed, is ignorant and has not mastered himself."[8]

"Of the three kinds of action," said Buddha, "the most heinous is not the word, not the physical act, but the thought."[4] From the moment of conception of an evil decision, man is already guilty, whether it be executed or not.

"The prime element in all is thought. Preponderant is thought, by thought all is made. If a man speaks or acts with evil thought, suffering follows him as the wheel follows the hoof of the beast that draws the cart.

"If a man speak or act with righteous thought, happiness follows him close as his never-absent shadow.

"Enemy works evil to enemy, hater to hater, but worse is the evil wrought by a wrongly directed mind." [8]

The Teacher pointed out vigilance over one's thoughts with especial insistence, because if the disciple, too confident of the results attained by him, were to lessen his vigilance, he would pay dearly for the slightest neglect. This advice was given in a parable: "A man was wounded with a poisoned arrow. The physician, having extracted the arrow, advised the wounded man to watch the wound most attentively. But the patient imagined he had nothing more to fear. Uncared for, the wound inflamed and caused death with acute pain." [4]

"Vigilance is the road to immortality. Negligence is the road to death. Those who are vigilant do not die. Those who are negligent are as if dead.

"To those who are inconstant in thought, ignorant of the true law, or wavering confidence, wisdom comes not to fullness.

"As a fletcher straightens his arrow, a wise man straightens his fickle and unsteady mind which is difficult to guard, difficult to guide.

"As rain leaks into an ill-thatched house, so craving leaks into an ill-trained mind.

"The great and small fetters of a bhikshu, who delights in vigilance and dreads negligence, are all burned away. He moves like fire." [8]

Indicating the madness, from the point of view of usefulness, of yielding to base inclinations, Buddha said:

"The feeling, for the sake of which you humiliated your-selves, will soon be only a memory to you, like a plea-sure experienced in a dream. But that which remains as a constant living reproach is the deed performed for this pleasure." [6]

"Morality is like an inflated leather bag, damage it once and it is destroyed. Likewise, succumb but once to vicious inclinations, and nothing can arrest the rush of passions. And a man left to himself will irrevocably perish."

"Irrigators deflect water where they will; fletchers shape the arrow; carpenters turn the wood to their will; the wise bend themselves." [8]

In the writings, we find no difference made between the members of the community—the social leaders the married, celibates, men, women—all may receive equally the Truth taught to them.

Admission into the community was not followed by any vows. The one who came brought with him only a readiness to serve the Teaching. But when this readiness disappeared, nothing bound him to remain in the com-munity. Leaving the community was as simple as admis-sion. Numerous are the examples of those who left the community and returned later.

One should not expel a member of the community merely because one does not agree with him in the appreciation of his deed. To expel him would mean to free the torrent of fiery words and disunion in the com-munity. "A member of the community will not repeat what he has heard so as to disunite others, but will bring them closer, pronouncing only the words of peace." [28]

"Never was hatred destroyed by hatred; goodness alone put an end to it; such is the eternal law.

"He abused me, he misused me, he overpowered me, he robbed me; in those who harbor such thoughts, anger is never stilled.

"If a man concern himself with the faults of others and is ever inclined to be offended, his own passions will grow, and he is far from the destruction of passions." [8]

"There are some who do not know the need of self-restraint; if they are quarrelsome, we may excuse their conduct. But those who know better should learn to live in concord.

"If a man finds a wise friend who lives righteously and is constant in his character, he may live with him, overcoming all dangers, happy and mindful. But ... with fools there is no companionship. Rather than to live with men who are selfish, vain, argumentative and obstinate, let a man walk alone." [9]

Influenced by goal-fitness in all things, Buddha did not strive to systematize his Teaching. He wished each point of the Teaching to affect as powerfully as possible the will of his disciples. Aiming only for the growth and development of consciousness he permitted freedom of thought and action in all else. Buddha desired individual discipline for each one.

"How did Buddha elect disciples for achievement? During work, when fatigue already possessed the disciples, Buddha asked the most unexpected question, awaiting the promptest reply.

"Or placing the simplest object before them he suggested that they describe it in not more than three words and not less than a hundred pages. Or placing a pupil before a sealed door he asked: 'How will you open it?'

"Or ordering musicians to perform beneath the window he made them sing hymns of entirely dissimilar contents.

"Or passing in front of the pupils he would ask them how many times he had done so.

"Or noticing an annoying fly he asked the pupil to repeat words unexpectedly pronounced.

"Or noticing a fear of animals or natural phenomena he set his pupils the condition to master it.

"Thus the powerful Lion tempered the blade of the spirit." (Written down from the oral teachings of Hindu Buddhism.)

And one should not forget the favorite pastime of Buddha with his disciples, during moments of rest. The Teacher cast into space one word on the basis of which the disciples built an entire thought. There is no wiser test of the condition of consciousness.

Buddha, through true knowledge and firm realization of the change of all that exists, tempered his pupils, arming them with courage, patience and compassion, training true warriors for the common welfare.

Especially numerous in the ancient writings are instances of complete contempt for that which makes life easy and conventionally pleasant.

The renunciation of everything personal gives birth to the sense of true freedom; from freedom is born joy;

from joy, satisfaction; from satisfaction, the sense of calmness and happiness.

Buddha found the way to the hearts of people not through miracles, but by practical teaching of the perfection of everyday life and by his personal example of great cooperation.

And so great was his tolerance and desire for close cooperation with people that he never spoke against their rites or beliefs. "Reverence your belief and never condemn the belief of others." In all cases he was not concerned with outer forms and tried only to give a broader understanding of the inner meaning, explaining it from a new point of view.

"While the Blessed One was staying at the bamboo grove near Rajagriha, he once met on his way Srigala, a householder, who, clasping his hands, turned to the four quarters of the world, to the zenith above, and to the nadir below. And the Blessed One, knowing that this was done according to the traditional religious superstition to avert evil, asked Srigala, 'Why do you perform these strange ceremonies?'

"Srigala said in reply, 'Do you think it strange that I protect my home against the influence of demons? I know that thou, O Gotama Sakyamuni, whom people call the Tathagata and the Blessed Buddha, wouldst fain tell me that incantations are of no avail and possess no saving power. But listen to me and know that in performing this rite I honor, reverence, and keep sacred the words of my father.'

"Then the Tathagata said, 'You do well, O Srigala,

to honor, reverence, and keep sacred the words of your father; and it is your duty to protect your home, your wife, your children, and your children's children against the baneful influences of evil spirits. I find no fault with the performance of your father's rite. But I find that you do not understand the ceremony. Let the Tathagata, who now speaks to you as a spiritual father and loves you no less than did your parents, explain to you the meaning of the six directions:

" 'To guard your home by mysterious ceremonies is not sufficient; you must guard it by good deeds. Turn to your parents in the east, to your Teachers in the south, to your wife and children in the west, to your friends in the north, and regulate the zenith of your religious relations above you, and the nadir of your servants below you.

" 'Such is the religion your father desires you to have, and the performance of the ceremony will remind you of your duties.'

"And Srigala looked up to the Blessed One with reverence as to his father and said, 'Truly, Gotama, thou are the Buddha, the Blessed One, the holy Teacher. I never knew what I was doing, but now I know. Thou hast revealed to me the truth that was hidden, as one who brings a lamp into the darkness. I take my refuge in the Enlightened Teacher, in the Truth that enlightens, and in the community of brethren who have found the Truth.' " [10]

From the very beginning of his activity he was convinced that a word pronounced at the fitting time and in its proper place was more convincing than any miracle in its psychic effect on man and his regeneration. He severely commanded his disciples not to manifest their acquired "miraculous" powers before those who were not acquainted with the principles inherent in such powers. Besides this, such manifestations are harmful for the possessor himself, exalting him above his surroundings and developing conceit in him.

An ordained disciple must not boast of superhuman perfection. The disciple who with evil intent and from covetousness boasts of a superhuman perfection, be it celestial visions or miracles, is no longer a disciple of the Sakyamuni. "I forbid you, O bhikshus, to employ any spells or supplications, for they are useless, since the law of Karma governs all things. He who attempts to perform miracles has not understood the Doctrine of the Tathagata." [13]

The word and power of conviction were the only weapons applied by the Teacher to influence people.

Nowhere do we ever find anger or indignation, only the austere affirmation of truth. "The Blessed One is perfect in the conduct of his speech" points out the disciple Sariputra.

"Like the earth, patiently enduring without sorrow or pleasure all things cast upon it pure and impure, so does Buddha, untouched, endure reverence as well as the disdain of men. Like water, purifying and refreshing all without distinction though they be just or evil, Buddha gives his compassion to foes and friends." [11]

Numerous are the visits and discourses of Buddha with his hearers on that which directly touched them, and the many-sided discussions of their obligations in relation to their families and social welfare. His distinction from other teachers and his greatest merit lie in the fact that, considering the duty of man from the point of view of vital usefulness, he tried to apply sensitive and uplifting feeling to the practical life.

This vital, practical side of the Teaching is beautifully expressed in the answer of the Blessed One to Anathapindika, a man of incalculable wealth, called "the supporter of orphans and the friend of the poor," who came to consult him.

Hearing that Buddha was stopping in the bamboo grove near Rajagriha, Anathapindika set out that very night to meet the Blessed One. And the Blessed One perceived at once the pure heart of Anathapindika and greeted him with words of comfort.

Anathapindika said, "I see that thou art the Buddha, the Blessed One, and I wish to open to thee my whole mind. Having listened to my words advise me what I shall do. My life is full of work, and having acquired great wealth, I am surrounded with cares. Yet I enjoy my work and apply myself to it with all diligence. Many people are in my employ and depend upon the success of my enterprises.

"Now I have heard your disciples praise the bliss of the hermit and denounce the unrest of the world. 'The Holy One,' they say, 'has given up his kingdom and his inheritance and has found the path of righteousness, thus setting an example to all the world of how to attain Nirvana.'

"My heart yearns to do what is right and to be a blessing to my fellow beings. Let me then ask you, Must I give up my wealth, my home, and my business enterprises, and, like thee, choose homelessness in order to attain the bliss of the righteous life?"

And the Buddha replied: "The bliss of the righteous life is attainable by everyone who walks in the noble eightfold path. He that is attached to wealth had better cast it away than allow his heart to be poisoned by it; but he who does not cleave to wealth, and who, possessing riches uses them rightly, will be a blessing to his fellow beings.

"I say to thee, remain in thy station of life and apply thyself with diligence to thy enterprises. It is not life and wealth and power that enslave men, but their attachment to life and wealth and power.

"The bhikshu who retires from the world to lead a life of leisure derives no profit. For a life of indolence is an abomination, and want of energy is to be despised. The Dharma of the Tathagata does not require that a man choose homelessness or resign the world, unless he feels called upon to do so; but the Dharma of the Tathagata requires each man to free himself from the illusion of self, to cleanse his heart, to give up his thirst for pleasure, and to lead a life of righteousness.

"And whatever men do, whether they remain in the world as artisans, merchants, and officers of the King, or retire from the world and devote themselves to a life of religious meditation, let them put their whole heart into their task, let them be diligent and energetic. And if they are like the lotus, which growing in water yet remains untouched by water, if they struggle in life without cherishing envy or hatred, if they live in the world a life, not of self but a life of truth, then surely joy, peace, and bliss will dwell in their minds." [13]

As vital and practical are the beautiful answers of the Blessed One to the questions of Simha, the warrior.

"At that time many distinguished citizens were sitting together assembled in the town hall and spoke in many ways in praise of the Buddha, of the Dharma, and of the Sangha. Simha, the general-in-chief, a disciple of the Niggantha sect, was sitting among them. And Simha thought: 'Truly, the Blessed One must be the Buddha, the Holy One. I will go and visit him.'

"Then Simha, the general, went to the place where the Niggantha chief, Nataputta, was; and having approached him, he said: 'I wish, Lord, to visit the samana Gotama.'

"Nataputta said: 'Why should you, Simha, who believe in the result of actions according to their moral merit, go to visit the samana Gotama, who denies the result of actions? The samana Gotama, O Simha, denies the result of actions; he teaches the doctrine of non-action; and in this doctrine he trains his disciples.'

"Then the desire to go and visit the Blessed One, which had arisen in Simha, the general, abated.

"Hearing again the praise of the Buddha, of the Dharma, and of the Sangha, Simha asked the Niggantha chief a second time; and again Nataputta persuaded him not to go.

"When a third time the general heard some men of

distinction extol the merits of the Buddha, the Dharma, and the Sangha, the general thought: 'Truly the samana Gotama must be the Holy Buddha. What are the Nigganthas to me, whether they give their consent or not? I shall go without asking their permission to visit him, the Blessed One, the Holy Buddha.'

"And Simha, the general, said to the Blessed One: 'I have heard, Lord, that the samana Gotama denies the result of actions; he teaches the doctrine of non-action, saying that the actions of sentient beings do not receive their reward, for he teaches annihilation and the contemptibleness of all things; and in this doctrine he trains his disciples. Teachest thou the doing away with the soul and the burning away of man's being? Pray tell me, Lord, do those who speak thus say the truth, or do they bear false witness against the Blessed One, passing off a spurious Dharma as thy Dharma?'

"The Blessed One said: 'There is a way, Simha, in which one who says so is speaking truly of me; on the other hand, Simha, there is a way in which one who says the opposite is speaking truly of me, too. Listen, and I will tell thee:

" 'I teach, Simha, the not-doing of such actions as are unrighteous, either by deed, or by word, or by thought; I teach the not-bringing about of all those conditions of heart which are evil and not good. However, I teach, Simha, the doing of such actions as are righteous, by deed, by word, and by thought; I teach the bringing about of all those conditions of heart which are good and not evil.

"'I teach, Simha, that all the conditions of heart which are evil and not good, unrighteous actions by deed, by word, and by thought, must be burnt away. He who has freed himself, Simha, from all those conditions of heart which are evil and not good, he who has destroyed them like a palm tree which is rooted out, so that they cannot grow up again, such a man has accomplished the eradication of self.

"'I proclaim, Simha, the annihilation of egotism, of lust, of ill will, of delusion. However, I do not proclaim the annihilation of forbearance, of love, of charity, and of truth.

"'I deem, Simha, unrighteous actions contemptible, whether they be performed by deed, or by word, or by thought; but I deem virtue and righteousness praiseworthy.'

"And Simha said: 'One doubt still lurks in my mind concerning the doctrine of the Blessed One. Will the Blessed One consent to clear the cloud away so that I may understand the Dharma as the Blessed One teaches it?'

"The Tathagata having given his consent, Simha continued: 'I am a soldier, O Blessed One, and am appointed by the king to enforce his laws and to wage his wars. Does the Tathagata, who teaches kindness without end and compassion for all sufferers, permit the punishment of the criminal? and further, does the Tathagata declare that it is wrong to go to war for the protection of our homes, our wives, our children, and our property? Does the Tathagata teach the doctrine of a complete self-surrender, so that I should suffer the evil doer to do what he pleases and yield submissively to him who threatens to take by violence what is my own? Does the Tathagata maintain that all strife, including such warfare as is waged for a righteous cause, should be forbidden?'

"The Buddha replied: 'He who deserves punishment must be punished, and he who is worthy of favor must be favored. Yet at the same time he teaches to do no injury to any living being but to be full of love and kindness. These injunctions are not contradictory, for whosoever must be punished for the crimes which he has committed, suffers his injury not through the ill will of the judge but on account of his evil-doing. His own acts have brought upon him the injury that the executor of the law inflicts. When a magistrate punishes, let him not harbor hatred in his breast, yet a murderer, when put to death, should consider that this is the fruit of his own act. As soon as he shall understand that the punishment will purify his soul, he will no longer lament his fate but rejoice at it.'

"And the Blessed One continued: 'The Tathagata teaches that all warfare in which man tries to slay his brother is lamentable, but he does not teach that those who go to war in a righteous cause after having exhausted all means to preserve the peace are blameworthy. He must be blamed who is the cause of war.

" 'The Tathagata teaches a complete surrender of self, but he does not teach a surrender of anything to those powers that are evil, be they men or gods or the elements of nature. Struggle must be, for all life is a struggle of some kind. But he that struggles should look to it lest he struggle in the interest of self against truth and righteousness.

" 'He who struggles in the interest of self, so that he himself may be great or powerful or rich or famous, will have no reward, but he who struggles for righteousness and truth, will have great reward, for even his defeat will be a victory.

" '*Self* is not a fit vessel to receive any great success; *self* is small and brittle and its contents will soon be spilt for the benefit, and perhaps also for the curse, of others.

" 'Truth, however, is large enough to receive the yearnings and aspirations of all *selves* and when the *selves* break like soap bubbles, their contents will be preserved and in the truth they will lead a life everlasting.

" 'He who goeth to battle, O Simha, even though it be in a righteous cause, must be prepared to be slain by his enemies, for that is the destiny of warriors; and should his fate overtake him he has no reason for complaint.

" 'But he who is victorious should remember the instability of earthly things. His success may be great, but be it ever so great the wheel of fortune may turn again and bring him down into the dust.

" 'However, if he moderates himself and, extinguishing all hatred in his heart, lifts his downtrodden adversary up and says to him, "Come now and make peace and let us be brothers," he will gain a victory that is not a transient success, for its fruits will remain forever.

" 'Great is a successful general, O Simha, but he who has conquered self is the greater victor.

" 'The doctrine of the conquest of self, O Simha, is

not taught to destroy the souls of men, but to preserve them. He who has conquered self is more fit to live, to be successful, and to gain victories than he who is the slave of self.

" 'He whose mind is free from the illusion of self, will stand and not fall in the battle of life.

" 'He whose intentions are righteousness and justice, will meet with no failure, but be successful in his enterprises and his success will endure.

" 'He who harbors in his heart love of truth will live and not die, for he has drunk the water of immortality.

" 'Struggle then, O general, courageously; and fight thy battles vigorously, but be a soldier of truth and the Tathagata will bless thee.'

"When the Blessed One had spoken thus, Simha, the general, said: 'Glorious Lord, glorious Lord! Thou hast revealed the truth. Great is the doctrine of the Blessed One. Thou, indeed, art the Buddha, the Tathagata, the Holy One. Thou art the teacher of mankind. Thou showest us the road of salvation, for this indeed is true deliverance. He who follows thee will not miss the light to enlighten his path. He will find blessedness and peace. I take my refuge, Lord, in the Blessed One, and in his doctrine, and in his brotherhood. May the Blessed One receive me from this day forth while my life lasts as a disciple who has taken refuge in him.'

"And the Blessed One said: 'Consider first, Simha, what thou doest. It is becoming that persons of rank like thyself should do nothing without due consideration.'

"Simha's faith in the Blessed One increased. He replied:

'Had other teachers, Lord, succeeded in making me their disciple, they would carry around their banners through the whole city of Vesali, shouting: "Simha, the general, has become our disciple!" For the second time, Lord, I take my refuge in the Blessed One, and in the Dharma, and in the Sangha; may the Blessed One receive me from this day forth while my life lasts as a disciple who has taken his refuge in him.'

"Said the Blessed One: 'For a long time, Simha, offerings have been given to the Nigganthas in thy house. Thou shouldst therefore deem it right also in the future to give them food when they come to thee on their alms-pilgrimage.'

"And Simha's heart was filled with joy. He said: 'I have been told, Lord: "The samana Gotama says: 'To me alone and to nobody else should gifts be given. My pupils alone and the pupils of no one else should receive offerings.' " But the Blessed One exhorts me to give also to the Nigganthas. Well, Lord, we shall see what is seasonable. For the third time, Lord, I take my refuge in the Blessed One, and in his Dharma, and in his fraternity.' " [13]

In all things he was influenced by goal-fitness. "What privileges could heaven give you? You must be conquerors here in this world, in the conditions in which you are now." [12]

Once a great disputer tried to embarrass Buddha by plying him with controversial questions. Buddha ceased to pay attention to him and spoke to the crowds around him: "This man wishes not that which he sees. He seeks what he does not see. He will seek long in vain. He is not satisfied by what he sees around him and his desires are limitless. Greetings to those who have renounced desire."

Buddha was affirmed as a doctrine of life, because the penetration of a high and goal-fitted Teaching into daily life marked a new era in the life of humanity. For the previous forbiddances and denials a positive and practical Teaching was substituted, in consequence of which the morality was raised to a higher standard.

. . . . .

To abstain from all that was negative and with full energy to prompt the positive and beautiful was ordained.

Suicide was especially condemned by Buddha as was the taking of any life. "All tremble when facing punishment, all fear death; judging others by yourself, slay not, neither cause to slay." [8]

"The bhikshu abstains from all taking of life; shuns taking the life of any living creature. Laying aside cudgel and sword he is mild and merciful, kind and compassionate toward every living creature." [28]

. . . . .

The consumption of alcohol was forbidden and also to cause the intoxication of others, because drunkenness leads to downfall, crime, madness, and ignorance, which is the main cause of a new and burdensome existence. The necessity of complete chastity for the achievement of full spiritual development was also pointed out. But to have one wife and to be loyal to her was regarded as a form of chastity. Polygamy was severely condemned by Gotama Buddha, as bred by ignorance.

The Teaching concerning the sanctity of marriage was beautifully expounded by the Blessed One in the parable "The Marriage Feast in Jambunada."

" 'The greatest happiness which a mortal man can imagine is the bond of marriage that ties together two loving hearts. But there is a greater happiness still: it is the embrace of truth. Death will separate husband and wife, but death will never affect him who has espoused the truth.

" 'Therefore be married unto the truth and live with the truth in holy wedlock. The husband who loves his wife and desires a union that shall be everlasting must be faithful to her so as to be like truth itself; and she will rely upon him and revere him and minister unto him. And the wife who loves her husband and desires a union that shall be everlasting must be faithful to him so as to be like truth itself; and he will place his trust in her, [he will honor her,] he will provide for her. Verily, I say unto you, [their wedlock will be holiness and bliss, and] their children will become like unto their parents and will bear witness to their happiness.

" 'Let no man be single, let every one be wedded in holy love to the truth. And when Mara, the destroyer, comes to separate the visible forms of your being, you will continue to live in the truth, and you will partake of the life everlasting, for the truth is immortal.' " [13]

The Teaching of Buddha did more for the liberation

and happiness of woman than any other teaching of India. "Woman," Gotama said, "can attain the highest degree of knowledge open to man—she can become an Arhat. [29] Freedom, which is beyond forms, cannot depend on sex, which belongs to the world of forms." Women played an important part in the communities and many of them were remarkable for their knowledge and striving.

We quote his answer to the question of the woman disciple Soma, "How can this condition which is difficult for the wise to attain be reached by a woman with her limited mind? When the heart is at rest, when the consciousness is unfolded, then truth is perceived. But if one will think I am a woman, or I am a man, or I am this or that, let Mara be his concern." [14]

"The gates of immortality are open to all beings. Who has ears, let him approach, let him hearken to the Teaching and have faith." [4]

. . . . .

Buddha indicated the absurdity of the prejudice that ascribes a growing authority to words, on account of their being reiterated by an increasing number of scholars. A true scholar is one who has attained the perfection of realization, not one who mumbles the formulas, previously rejected, numbers of times.

"I say to my pupils, 'Here is Nirvana, here is the path to it.' Of those instructed by me, a few attain, others do not. What can I do? The Blessed One is only the Indicator of the path." [4]

"No man can save his neighbor. The evil committed

by man stains only the man himself. The evil avoided by him concerns him alone. Everyone is pure or impure for himself only. No man can purify another." [8]

Recovery is possible only through an inner process of work upon oneself. Therefore Buddha did not acknowledge any active power behind formulas transmitted from generation to generation, "like a basket transmitted from hand to hand." [4]

. . . . .

Buddha, denying the conventional concept of God and affirming the possibility of liberation entirely by personal efforts and assiduous labor upon oneself, by this alone refuted outer worship. From the very beginning, he censured all rituals and other outer actions, which only help the recrudescence of spiritual blindness and clinging to lifeless forms. Nowhere in his Teaching is there even a hint of personal worship. He said: "The Teaching is salvation not because it was given by Buddha but because it liberates. The pupil who follows me, clinging to the edge of my garment, is far from me and I from him. Why? Because this disciple does not see me. Another one may live hundreds of miles distant from me and in spite of this be close to me and I to him. Why? Because this disciple understands the Teaching; understanding the Teaching, he understands me." [15]

"If you understood and perceived the truth as it is, would you say, 'We owe respect to our Teacher, and out of respect for him, we shall speak as the Teacher spoke'?

" 'No, Blessed One.'

"That which you affirm is it not that which you perceived and realized yourself?

" 'Yes, Blessed One.' " [4]

Foreseeing the future, Buddha said: "The Teaching is like the flame of a torch, kindling innumerable fires. Those fires may be used for the cooking of food or to disperse the darkness, but the flame of the first torch remains invariably luminous." [16]

Being an enemy of all ritual, Buddha denied the purifying power of bathing. "A man will not become morally pure through cleansing himself lengthily in water. A pure man, a Brahmin, is one in whom abide truth and virtue." [17] "The Gaya is the same sort of reservoir as any other reservoir." [4]

"All your rules," said Buddha to the fanatics, "are base and ridiculous. Some of you walk naked, covering yourselves only with your hands; some will not eat out of a jug or a plate, will not sit at the table between two speakers, between two knives, or two plates; some will not sit at the common table and will not accept alms in a house where there is a pregnant woman, or where you notice many flies or meet a dog.

"One nurtures himself only on vegetables, with a brew of rice, with cow or deer dung, roots of trees, branches, leaves, forest fruit or seeds. One wears his robe thrown only over the shoulder, or covers himself only with moss, the bark of a tree, plants or reindeer skin, wears his hair loose or puts on a hair band. One wears the garment of sorrow, always holds his hands up, does not sit on a bench or mat, or always sits in the manner of an animal.

"One lies on prickly plants or cow dung.

"I shall not enumerate other similar means by which you torture and exhaust yourselves.

"What do you expect, voluntary laborers, for your heavy work? You expect alms and respect from laymen, and when you attain this aim you become strongly attached to the comforts of temporary life, you do not want to part with it and do not know the means for it. As soon as you notice visitors from afar you at once sit down and pretend to be absorbed in deep meditation, but after they depart you again do as you please, walk and rest freely.

"When given coarse food, without even tasting it you give it back, but each tasty morsel you keep for yourselves. Indulging in vices and passions you nevertheless garb yourselves in the mask of modesty. No, not such is the true achievement!

"Asceticism is useful only when it does not conceal covetous motives."

Asceticism has no value as a means of liberation from the bonds of Earth. It is more difficult to find a patient man than one who nurtures himself with air and roots or garbs himself in bark and leaves. "When a man is weakened by hunger and thirst, when he is too tired to master his feelings and thoughts, can he reach the goal which is attained only by the clear mind of an expanded consciousness?" [18]

"In order that the strings of the vina should produce a harmonious sound, they should be neither too strained nor too loose. So with each effort: if it is excessive, it ends in a futile waste of energy; if it is niggardly, it turns into passivity.

"Practice measurement; keep the correct measure in tensity and establish the balance of your abilities.

"A disciplined man is free; being free, he is joyous, he is calm and happy." [4] Buddha wanted the life of the community to be joyous.

When he formulated the precepts for his son, he commanded him to treasure joy together with love, compassion and patience.

IN BUDDHISM, a man is capable of a virtue only if he has cognizance of it. One cannot despair of a man creating evil, if he knows what he does. He sees wrong, but at least he sees. Having achieved some knowledge, he can renounce his former deeds. But what may one expect of a man possessed of mental blindness? "Of two people who have committed the same error, he is worse who does not realize it. Of two innocent persons, he is better who realizes that he is not guilty. For one cannot expect a man who does not consider himself guilty to manifest effort for the cessation of his erring." [4]

In order to cure oneself, one has to know one's ailment, but the realization of it does not give health; for that, the necessary condition is a manifestation of will.

Considering all existing manifestations as correlations of most refined energies, the Teacher valued especially the evidence of effort in his pupils. He never taught the subjugation of passions, as such, but the transmutation and the sublimation of their quality, for at the base of each passion is contained the spark of energy without which no progress is possible.

Energy and will make the pupil vigilant and full of constant striving. These qualities arm him with patience, energy, sustained control—three indispensable conditions to crush the hordes of Mara, "as an elephant crushes a bamboo hut." [14] Patience is born of compassion and knowledge.

Of intolerance, it is pointed out that "The mistakes

of others are easily noticed, but one's own mistakes are perceived with difficulty. A man sifts the misdeeds of his neighbor like the grain from the husk, but hides his own as the cheat hides the bad dice from the player." [8]

Nowhere do we see mention of non-resistance to evil, but everywhere, active condemnation and suppression of evil. One should not submit to suffering, one must be daring in the perfection of good and not be satisfied with small achievements. "Like a beautiful flower, full of color but without scent, so are the fine but fruitless words of him who does not act in accordance with them." [8]

"I indicated to my disciples the path which they must tread in order to manifest the four perfect efforts: to prevent the beginning of the harmful, evil thing if it be not yet manifested; to hinder its development if it be already manifested; to help the manifestation of useful things not yet manifested; and to strengthen those which are already manifested. Thus the disciple creates will, striving, develops courage, exercises the heart and fights." [4]

We can never call Buddha mild. On the contrary, he is the never-despondent Leader, the Fighter for community and for matter, the Hero of work and unity.

Buddha pointed out the necessity of co-measurement and goal-fitness. He said: "One should be neither less nor more." His followers made of this formula of co-measurement the tiresome golden mean. But the golden mean, or the middle path, should be understood as the realization of harmony. Buddha likewise commanded the possession of fewer objects, in order not to allot too much time to them. This advice his followers transformed into pedantry. Buddha censured fanatics and advised that the body be treated according to the necessity of conditions. Where the body should be reduced for travel, the Teacher pointed out slenderness. But where the contagion of the atmosphere necessitated protection, the Teacher ordained food. In the Teaching of Buddha we find not only a philosophy of Matter but also the practical improvement of daily life.

The Teacher pointed out the necessity of harmony in man's forces, for the manifestation of the highest measure of knowledge and beauty, and for the scientifically vital necessity of cosmic economy for the general good.

"He will observe co-measurement in clemency, and, being resourceful in means, he will combine wisdom with compassion." [5]

"The charitable man has found the path of salvation. He is like a man who plants a sapling, thereby insuring shade, flowers and fruit for future years. Just so is the result of charity, just so is the joy of him who helps those that are in need of assistance. Just so is the great Nirvana.

"Immortality can be reached only by continuous acts of kindness; and perfection is accomplished by compassion and charity."

Goal-fitness and compassion are vividly expressed in the following dialogue:

"Does the Blessed One pronounce a word which is false, destructive and disagreeable?"

"No."

"If it is true, destructive, and disagreeable?"

"Also not."

"If true, useful and disagreeable?"

"Yes, when he finds it necessary."

"If it be false, destructive, and agreeable?"

"No."

"True, useful, and agreeable?"

"Yes, when he finds the time befitting."

"Why does he act thus?"

"Because he has compassion toward all beings."[7]

Many indications about the evidences of compassion are contained in the Sutras; one does not need to enumerate them, because all the refinement and the touching relation of Buddha to his neighbor are contained in the last episode:

Chunda, the smith, hearing that Buddha had come to Pava and was stopping in the grove, went to him and, paying him reverence, asked the Blessed One to partake of his meal on the following day. Receiving his acceptance, Chunda departed and prepared all possible delicacies and also a large piece of juicy pork for the following morning. The Blessed One accompanied by his disciples came to the home of the smith. Sitting down on the prepared seat, he addressed Chunda, the smith:

"Chunda, bring me the pork thou hast preserved, but to the disciples give the other delicacies prepared by thee."

"Yes, Lord," replied the smith, and executed what was told.

Then the Blessed One said: "Chunda, bury whatever

is left of the pork, for I know no being besides the Tathagata who could digest it."

"Yes, Lord," answered Chunda, and he buried the remains of the pork in the ground.

Having partaken of food in the house of Chunda, the smith, the Blessed One was stricken with severe sickness of the stomach and suffered terrible pain. He said to his disciple, Ananda, "Arise, Ananda, we shall go to Kusinara." On the way the Blessed One stopped often, suffering great pain, thirst, and anguish. Thus they reached the river Kakutshta. Having bathed here, the Blessed One stopped at the outskirts of the grove and, lying down on an outspread robe, said to Ananda: "Ananda, it is possible that someone may harass the heart of Chunda, the smith, by saying: 'Chunda, what distress for thee! Thou must feel very unhappy that the Tathagata left the illusory world after he accepted the meal in thy house.'

"Ananda, dispel the heavy thoughts of Chunda by the following words: 'Friend, thou must rejoice, for thy happiness lies in that this happened in such a manner. From the lips of Tathagata himself, I have heard and understood that two gifts of food receive equal appreciation and reward—verily, they receive a greater reward and blessing than any other. Which two? That, after which a Tathagata attains the highest and complete enlightenment and that, after partaking of which, he enters the liberation of Nirvana.' With such words, Ananda, should you dissipate the heavy thoughts of Chunda, the smith." [19]

. . . . .

The more deeply we penetrate into the Teaching of the Blessed One, the more vividly appear his boundless compassion and love, which permeate each of his thoughts and actions.

"Like a mother who protects her only child with her own life, cultivate such boundless love toward all beings!"[7]

His all-embracing sympathy with all existing things extends even to the vegetable kingdom. He avoids destroying seeds and plantlife. In the *Anguttara Nikaya* the Blessed One says, "Whoever of my disciples cultivates mind-delivering love but for a moment, that disciple meditates not in vain and follows the Doctrine and the discipline of the Teacher; how much more do those who cultivate the thought of love!"

In the *Itivuttaka* it is said, "All methods for the earning of merit in this life are not worth one-sixteenth part of love, the deliverance of mind. Love, the deliverance of mind, takes them into itself, shining and glowing and beaming.

"And as the shining of all the stars does not equal one-sixteenth of the brightness of the moon, but as moonlight absorbs it into itself, shining and glowing and beaming, so all methods for the earning of merit in this life are not worth one-sixteenth part of love, the deliverance of the mind.

"Love, the deliverance of the mind, takes them into itself, shining, glowing and beaming.

"And as in the last month of the rainy season in autumn the sun in a clear and cloudless sky, mounting the firmament, clears away all darkness in the expanse of air, shining and glowing and beaming; and as, following the night, early in the morning the morning star shines and glows and beams, even so all means for the earning of merit in this life are not worth one-sixteenth part of love, the deliverance of mind. Love, the deliverance of mind, takes them into itself, shining and glowing and beaming."

Buddha's love was of so immeasurable a stream that it could not be exhausted by any hate or hostility. On the contrary, such a hostile attack only brought it to fuller unfoldment. Therefore, he decreed that his disciples act thus, "However men may speak concerning you, whether appropriately or inappropriately, whether courteously or rudely, whether wisely or foolishly, whether kindly or maliciously, thus, my disciples, must you train yourselves. Our minds should remain unsullied; neither should evil word escape our lips. Kind and compassionate will we ever remain, loving of heart, not harboring secret hate. And we will bathe them with the unfailing stream of loving thought. And proceeding further, we will embrace and flood the whole wide world with constant thoughts of loving kindness, wide, ample, expanding, immeasurable as the world, free from enmity, free from ill will. Thus, disciples, must you train yourselves!"[4]

Here we see that the love that his disciples had to cultivate was the boundless stream of kindness radiating to all four quarters of space, above and below, in all places the wide world over.

According to the Teaching these waves of kindness,

compassion, or joy sent into space reach a mind afflicted with sorrow and grief, which suddenly feels within itself a welling-up of peace and serenity.

Thought is energy and as such acts in full conformity with its intensity and the impetus given to it.

Love, as taught by the Blessed One, being the deliverance of mind, was at the root of everything really great.

"The greatest of all is the loving heart." [2]

ONE MORE LEGEND from Buddha's life. "The Blessed One sat above the waters of a deep lake. In its depths one could discern an entire world of fish and seaweeds. The Blessed One noticed how this small world resembled the courts of royalty, 'If man should sink there, he would destroy these ephemeral dwellings with his feet, but he himself would choke. Out of such depths the spirit of man does not arise.'

" 'But,' smiled the Teacher, 'for everything there is a remedy. One can shatter the rock and drain the lake. The snails will then have either to dry up or to find another place of existence. But man will not perish.' "

. . . . .

In Buddhist writings six teachers, philosophers, are often mentioned as Buddha's constant antagonists. Those were the philosophers who disputed the theoretical bases of Buddha's Teaching. Two hypotheses in the Teaching of Gotama Buddha were especially subject to attack: his Teaching about causes and his denial of an independent and unchangeable soul in man and in the Universe—the very hypotheses which are so close to our contemporary trend of thought.

Affirming the reality which surrounds us and is visible to all, the Teacher pointed out the existence of the most subtle reality, which is attainable only through higher knowledge. The knowledge of this reality and the possession of this higher knowledge are usually imperceptible to our coarse sense organs.

"If that which is realized by our feelings existed as the only reality, then the fool, by right of birth, would possess the fundamental Truth; what, then, would be the use of all quests for the realization of the essence of things?"

In our brains are centers, the opening of which gives the possibility of possessing immutable knowledge. In this affirmation we again see how the Teacher proceeded in a purely scientific direction, coinciding in this statement with the affirmations of contemporary scientists concerning the many centers in our organism, the functions of which are yet unknown but which, according to the importance of the places they occupy, one may suppose to be of unusual significance.

The idea of God has its own interpretation for Buddhists, in accordance with the law of Karma and with the understanding of the necessity of personal efforts for one's own liberation. "Who is it that shapes our lives? Is it Ishvara, a personal creator? If Ishvara be the maker, all living things should have silently to submit to their maker's power. They would be like vessels formed by the potter's hand; and if it were so, how would it be possible to practice virtue? If the world had been made by Ishvara there should be no such thing as sorrow, or calamity, or sin; for both pure and impure deeds must issue from him. If not, there would be another cause besides him, and he would not be self-existent. Thus, thou seest, the thought of Ishvara is overthrown.

"Again, it is said that the Absolute has created us. But that which is absolute cannot be a cause. All things around us come from a cause as the plant comes from the seed; but how can the Absolute be the cause of all things alike? If it pervades them, then, certainly, it does not make them.

"Again, it is said that *Self* is the maker. But if *Self* is the maker, why did he not make things pleasing? The cause of sorrow and joy are real and objective. How can they have been made by *Self*?

"Again, if we adopt the argument that there is no maker, our fate is such as it is, and there is no causation, what use would there be in shaping our lives and adjusting means to an end?

"Therefore, we argue that all things that exist are not without cause. However, neither Ishvara, nor the Absolute, nor the Self, nor causeless chance, is the maker, but our deeds produce results both good and evil." [13]

"The whole world is under the law of causation and causes that are mental and not mental—the gold of which the cup is made is gold throughout. Let us not lose ourselves in vain speculations about profitless subtleties; let us surrender Self and selfishness, and since all things are fixed by causation, let us practice good so that good may result from our actions." [2]

If the eternally changing existence of man excludes the hypothesis of a constant, changeless entity, then the Universe, this complex of complexes, may be explained entirely without the necessity or even the possibility of introducing into it an unchanging and eternal Being.

Two doctrines were especially condemned by Buddha:

1. The affirmation of the eternal unchanging soul.
2. The destruction of the soul after death.

Both these doctrines were denied by the law of causal conception, which establishes that all dharmas are at the same time causes and consequences.

Buddha denied the existence of a changeless soul in man and in everything, for he saw in man and the whole Universe only inconstancy and the transitional.

The thesis of *the continuity of the stream of phenomena* and the formula of *the causality of conception* exclude the existence of the eternal unchanging soul, individual as well as universal.

The connotation of the words *unchanging soul* is absolutely inadmissible for the Buddhist; because the thought that man can be a being separated from all other beings and from the existence of the whole Universe, can neither be proved by logic nor supported by science. "In this world no one is independent. All that exists depends on causes and conditions." "Each thing depends upon another thing and the thing it depends upon is, in turn, not independent."[6]

Buddha constantly taught that there is no independent "I" and that there is no world separated from it. There are no independent things, there is no separate life—all are only indissoluble correlatives. If there is no separate "I," we cannot say that this or that is mine, and thus the origin of the understanding of property is destroyed.

If the understanding of a permanent and independent human soul is to be rejected, what, then, in man gives him the sense of a permanent personality? The answer will be—*trishna*, or the craving for existence. A being who has generated causes for which he is responsible and possesses this craving, will, according to his karma, be born anew.

Of one and the same complex of elements (dharmas) are born infinite combinations of skandhas —elements, which are manifested at the given time as one personality, and after a definite period of time appear as another, third, fourth, etc., *ad infinitum*. There occurs, not a transmigration, but an endless transformation of a complex of dharmas, or elements—that is, a continuous regrouping of the elements—substrata which form the human personality.

Upon the quality of the new combination of skandhas—elements of the new personality—the last desire before death of the previous personality has a great influence: it gives direction to the liberated stream.

In Buddhism a man is regarded as an individuality, built by numerous existences, but only partially manifested in each new appearance on the earthly plane.

The individual existence, consisting of an entire chain of lives, which began, continue, and finish in order to begin again, *ad infinitum*, is compared to a wheel or a year of twelve months, invariably repeated. The chain of the Twelve Nidanas becomes no longer a chain, but the Wheel of Life, with twelve spokes. Once set in motion, the Wheel of Life, the Wheel of the Law, will never stop: "The Wheel of the Benevolent Law in its unchange-able rotation crushes untiringly the worthless chaff, separating it from the golden grain. The hand of Karma directs the Wheel, its revolutions marking the beat of its heart."

All these changes of forms or of existence lead toward one goal—the attainment of Nirvana; it means the full development of all possibilities contained in the human organism. But Buddhism teaches the cognizance and creation of good, independent of this aim, since the contrary would be absolute egoism, and such speculation is foredoomed to disappointment. As it is said, Nirvana is the epitome of disinterestedness, complete renunciation of all that is personal for the sake of truth. An ignorant man dreams and strives to Nirvana, without any realization of its true essence. To create good with the view of gaining results or to lead a disciplined life for the attainment of liberation is not the noble path ordained by Gotama. Without thought of reward or achievement life must be crossed, and such a life is the greatest.

The state of Nirvana may be attained by man in his earthly life.

. . . . .

Buddhism recognizes no difference between the physical and psychic worlds. Reality attributed to the action of thought is of the same order as reality of objects cognized by our senses. Said the Blessed One: "Verily I say unto you, your mind is mental, but that which you perceive with your senses is also mental. There is nothing within or without the world that either is not mind or cannot become mind. There is spirituality in all existence, and the very clay upon which we tread can be changed into children of truth." [13]

Buddhism regards all existing phenomena as one reality. Physically and psychically these phenomena are dharmas, objects of our cognizance. Within us and without, we come in touch only with dharmas, for in us and outside us exist only dharmas. The word *dharma* is one of the most significant and most difficult to translate in the Buddhist terminology. Dharma is a manifold factor, a factor of consciousness with an inherent property of definite expression. Our organs give us sensations which are transformed into dharmas through the action of cognizance. Ideas, images, and all intellectual processes are, first of all, dharmas.

As color, form, and sound are to the eye and ear, so dharmas are to the consciousness. They exist for us by their effects. "The color blue exists only to the extent that we receive the sensation of blue."

It is customary to call the Teaching of Buddha itself, Dharma, since *dharma* also signifies *law*.

Subjective and objective phenomena are continuously changing. They are real; but their reality is momentary, because all that exists is but part of an eternally unfolding development—dharmas appear one moment, in order to change in the next. This doctrine of the eternal flux of all things was so fundamental a characteristic of the Teaching that it was even named "The Theory of Instantaneous Destruction."

Dharmas (transcendental bearers of definite qualities) are drawn into the stream of eternal change of vibrations. Their combinations define the specifications of objects and individuals. Only that which is beyond combinations is unchangeable. The ancient teaching knew only one concept which was integral, unconditioned, and eternal—Nirvana.

Every dharma is a cause, for every dharma is energy. If this energy is inherent in each conscious being, it manifests itself in a twofold way: outwardly, as the immediate cause of phenomena; inwardly, by transmuting the one who has engendered it and by containing in itself the consequences revealed in the near or distant future.

We find that the physical and psychic organism of a man is but the combination of five groups of aggregates, or skandhas, which are divided into physical qualities:

1. form—*rupa*;
2. feelings—*vedana*;
3. perceptions—*samjna*;
4. forces—*samskara*;
5. consciousness—*vijnana*.

All five are equally unstable and dual. Samskara are the inclinations and creative powers, explaining the present dharmas by the previous ones and indicating which of the present dharmas prepare those of the future.

"Samskara are accumulations left by former sensations and lend their fragrance to future sensations." From this definition of samskara-skandha it is clear that this group of elements appears as the one absorbing all the peculiarities of the other skandhas. Samskara skandhas (causal body)—the preservation of this group of skandhas is conditioned by the necessity of manifesting; when this necessity disappears, they are transformed into pure light. Vijnana-skandha and partly samjna lend their coloring, or character, to the other combinations, and therefore appear as the cause defining the next existence, in the sense of strivings and inclinations.

"Rupa is like a plate; vedana is like food contained in the plate; samjna is like a sauce; samskara is like the cook, and vijnana is like the eater." Said the Blessed One: "It is by a process of evolution that sankharas come to be. There is no sankhara which has sprung into being without a gradual becoming. Thy sankharas are the product of thy deeds in former existences. The combination of thy sankharas is thy self. Wheresoever they are impressed thither thy self migrates. In thy sankharas thou wilt continue to live and thou wilt reap in future existences the harvest sown now and in the past." [13]

No element carries from one existence into another, but not one attains a new existence without having had its cause in the previous existence. When the old consciousness ceases to exist, it is death. When consciousness returns to existence, a new birth takes place. One should understand that the present consciousness is not born of the old consciousness, but that its present state is the result of causes accumulated in the previous existence.

From one life to another there is no transmission, but there is a seeming reflection, solidarity.

"The man who sows is not he who reaps; yet he is not also another man."

The content of consciousness consists of dharmas. Dharmas are thoughts. These thoughts are as real as the four elements or the organs of sense, because from the moment a thing is thought, it already exists. Man is a complex of combinations and at each moment his nature is defined by the amount and quality of the particles of which he is composed. Each change in his combination makes a new being of him. But this change does not exclude continuity because the motion of skandhas does not occur accidentally or beyond the law. Drawn into the eternal ebb and flow, the aggregates change in one direction or in another, as the conditions of each new combination are defined by a cause; and this cause is the quality of the preceding cause. Each successive combination harvests the fruit of former combinations and plants the seed which will bear fruit in the future combinations.

Man is a complex of combinations and at the same time he is the link. He is the complex because at each moment he contains a great number of skandhas; he is the link because between the two successive conditions there is at the same time the difference and solidarity. "If there were no difference, milk would not turn into curdled milk. And if there were no solidarity, there would be no need in milk to have curdled milk."

Let us explain by one more example: Physiologically

the human organism completely changes every seven years, and yet when the man A is forty years of age he is absolutely identical with the eighteen-year-old youth A; nevertheless, on account of the constant destruction and rebuilding of his body and changes in his mind and character, he is a different being. A man in his old age is the precise consequence of the thoughts and deeds of each preceding stage of his life. Likewise, the new personality, being the previous individuality, but in a changed form, in a new combination of the skandhas—elements, justly reaps the consequences of the thoughts and deeds of his former existences.

The consciousness and its eternally changing contents are one. "There is no permanent 'I,' which would remain unchangeable."—"It is necessary that the embryo should die in order that a child may be born; the death of the child is needed in order that the boy may be born, and the death of the boy produces the youth." [5]

It is customary to compare human existence with a necklace—each bead is one of the physical manifestations. But perhaps it is clearer to conceive of this evolution as a complex mixture into which, with each new embodiment on the earthly plane, a new ingredient is being added which naturally changes the whole mixture.

Each new manifestation is limited by physical elements, rupa-skandha.

· · · · ·

The energy striving to create a new being and directed by karma is called "trishna"—the stimulus, the craving for existence.

And this stimulus, when imbued with the essence of the Teaching, rises before us not only as the greatest cosmic principle but also as the greatest and most beautiful cosmic mystery. And Gotama Buddha, who unceasingly pointed out the eternally rushing stream of our lives, has thus asserted the cosmicality and, consequently, the infinity of this stimulus, which many who misquote the Teaching try to suppress; but the fiery spirit of the Teacher could only destroy small concepts, broadening them into infinity. And Nirvana is the Gate that introduces us into the rhythm of the highest, fiery, creative, and eternally expanding stream of infinite Existence.

The Teaching of Buddha is an untiring fiery call to the realization of the beauty and unity of the great creativeness of infinite Existence.

WHAT IS KARMA? The action of the consequences of that which is done by man—in deed, word, and thought. The inner effect, as pointed out previously, manifests itself only in conscious beings. Hence, the colossal responsibility of man before all that exists and, first of all, before himself. "That which I call karma is only thought; for, having thought, man acts through his body, word, and mind." [20] Karma is created by thoughts. "There is no merit for the one who gives gold thinking he gives a stone." The tendency of thought gives man his moral value, changed by deeds in one direction or another.

"A good action is manifested and completed. And even though it may no longer exist, nevertheless its consequence exists. At the moment of action a definite combination of dharmas arises in the 'stream' of this man." In this is contained the indestructibility of the deed. Thus, to the purely mechanical understanding of cause and effect, Buddhism adds also responsibility. One of such combinations, aggregates, which we call an individual is defiled or uplifted by the actions of the preceding combination with which it is solidary. "I teach nothing but Karma." [21]

The persistence which Buddha exerted in order to instill into his disciples the understanding of moral responsibility resulting from the law of Karma, proves that herein was contained the fact of primary Truth, self-contained and absolute, Truth which must guide all the actions of man. "To doubt the moral power of a deed means to close our eyes to evidence."

"All beings have their karma. They are the heirs of deeds and the sons of deeds. They are completely dependent upon their deeds. Deeds establish differences of low and superior conditions between beings."[4]

"Verily, out of that which was is being created that which is. Man is born according to what he has created. All beings have karma as their heritage."[4]

"Not only is the correspondence between fruit and seed exact, but action, like every good seed, expands a hundredfold."

Each man, by the action of unerring karma, receives in exact measure all that is due, all that he deserves, neither more nor less. Not one benevolent or evil action, trifling as it may be, as secretly as it may be done, escapes the precisely balanced scale of karma. Karma is causality, acting on the moral as well as on the physical and other planes. Buddhists say there are no miracles in human deeds, what man has sown he will reap. "There exists no place on earth or in heaven or under the water, nor is there a place in the depths of the mountains, where evil action does not bring suffering to him who begot it.

"If a man offend a harmless and innocent person, the evil blows back upon that fool, like light dust thrown up against the wind.

"An evil that is committed, like newly drawn milk, does not curdle at once. It follows the fool closely like a smoldering spark that at last breaks into burning flame."[8]

. . . . .

A foolish man, learning that the Buddha observed the principle of great love which commends the return of good for evil, came and abused him. Buddha was silent, pitying his folly.

After the man had finished his abuse, Buddha asked him, "Son, if a man declines a gift made to him, to whom would it belong?" And he answered, "In that case it would belong to the man who offered it."

"My son," said Buddha, "You have railed at me, but I refuse to accept your abuse and request you to keep it yourself. Will it not be a source of misery to you? As the echo belongs to the sound and the shadow to the substance, so will misery overtake the evildoer without fail.

"A wicked man who reproaches a virtuous one is like a man who looks up and spits at heaven; the spittle does not soil the heaven, but comes back and defiles his own person.

"The slanderer is like one who casts dust at another when the wind is contrary; the dust only returns on him who cast it. The virtuous man cannot be hurt, and the misery that the other desires to inflict comes back upon himself." [16]

. . . . .

Buddha's tolerance—honor thy own faith, but never slander that of others.

In general, people return to Earth until their consciousness outgrows the earthly level. Buddha pointed out that there existed whole systems of worlds of different grades—the highest and lowest—and that the inhabitants of each world correspond to each other in their development. The world in which the appointed man must be manifested as well as the quality of the reincarnation itself are determined by the predominance in him of positive or negative qualities, in other words, in scientific language—the birth will be controlled by his true attractions, or by his karma, according to Buddhists.

Like a misdeed, remorse is an action. And this action has consequences, which can balance the consequence of the misdeed. Buddha said, "If a man who committed evil realizes his fault, is remorseful and creates good, the power of his chastisement will gradually be exhausted, like a fever which gradually loses its destructive effect in proportion to the perspiration of the patient." [16]

Karma is thought; therefore, the quality of thinking may change or even completely liberate man from the effects of karma. If deeds accumulated one upon another, man would be encircled by his karma as in a conjured circle. But by teaching that there is a state of consciousness which can destroy the reaction of committed deeds, Buddha pointed out the possibility of cessation of human suffering. Will and energy are rulers of karma. From all that was said it is clear that the law of Karma and the law of reincarnation are inseparable, for one is the logical consequence of the other.

AMONG SOME WESTERN scholars it has been an accepted opinion to regard Buddhism as the Teaching of despair and inaction, which does not at all correspond to its fundamental character.

Buddha, as the true Leader of general good, fearlessly revealed to humanity the real dangers of existence and at the same time showed the way to avoid them—this way is knowledge. Who may call the man who halts you at the edge of the precipice a pessimist?

"Beings live in a house surrounded by flames; nevertheless they feel no fear nor awe. They do not know; they are frivolous; they are not frightened; they do not try to save themselves; they seek enjoyment and roam about in different directions in this triple world, similar to a house ensnared by flames." [22]

"The fools think that suffering lies only in sensations of pain. Verily their feelings are distorted. They are like a sick man who imagines that sugar is bitter. A fluff of wool settling on the hand is imperceptible, but entering the eye, it causes severe pain. The palm is like an ignorant man, the eye is like a sage. Only the sage is deeply affected by the spectacle of the suffering of the world." [23]

If after such statements anyone could call Buddha a pessimist, he would be like those ignorant people who kill the doctors that come to make healing inoculations. And the same people, inclined to ascribe to the Teaching the keynote of despair, cite the affirmation of Buddha,

"I am the destroyer of old age and death. I am the best physician. I possess the highest means." [24]

"Drink, laboring ones, drink the remedy of Truth and, partaking of it, live. Having absorbed it you will conquer old age and death." [24]

We quote an authoritative opinion of the chief abbot of the monastery Kamakura Soyen-Shaku, "Buddhism is the most rational and intellectual teaching in the world." [25]

The Teaching of Buddha, impregnated in its very structure with the affirmation of the self-contained human entity in its cosmic scope of striving toward far-off worlds, is full of true greatness and beauty.

Naturally the question may arise—how did the Teacher recall beauty in its earthly manifestations? It is pointed out that even at the hour of death the thoughts of the Teacher were directed toward the beautiful, remembering the beauty of the best places he traversed. "Beautiful is Rajagriha, the Vulture's Peak, the Robber's Cliff; beautiful are the groves and mountains." "Vaishali, what a place of beauty!" [19]

ALL ANCIENT PHILOSOPHICAL teachings affirmed the law of Karma and the law of final liberation, but the value of the Teaching of Buddha lies in the fact that without infringing upon the basis of all these scientific and philosophic theses, it turned to Earth, to earthly labor, pointing out that only by the way of real, strenuous labor and self-development can one achieve true progress; thus he affirmed the evolution of humanity as an organic part of the Cosmos.

The word *stream*, so often used by Buddha in its application to the Cosmos and human existence, is nothing other than the concept expressed by our word *evolution*.

"The contact of cosmic transformation with psychic energy gives birth to the condition of a successful stream." Thus spoke Buddha.

Even as previous Teachings may be characterized as an estrangement from Earth, so Buddha appears as a true ploughman of our Earth, laying the foundation of conscious and real labor. In his case the formula, "by human hands and feet," can be applied. And in this is contained the unrepeatable uniqueness of the value of the Teaching and the labor of Gotama Buddha.

There does not exist a more beautiful appeal to the world than this constantly repeated affirmation: "Brothers, I do not come to offer you any dogmas, and I do not ask you to believe in that which so many others believe. I only exhort you to independent enlightenment, to use your own mind, developing it instead of letting it become dull. I adjure you not to resemble beasts of prey or stupid sheep. I implore you to be men with right views, men who toil untiringly for the acquisition of real knowledge, which will prevail over suffering."

We are not interested in the latest additions which surround Buddhism, only the foundations ordained by the Teacher himself are needed for the future. And in these foundations one can see the Teaching, not only laid out with an iron will but impressed with the steps of his lengthy wanderings.

One is astonished at the arguments with which superficial investigators have supported their opinion of the Teaching of Buddha as one of despair. This is a falsehood! It is the song of the greatness of labor, the song of the victory of humanity, the song of austere joy.

The Teaching of Buddha may be called the experiment of a working community.

Not only the Buddhist understanding, but all just minds as well, must value the stone of Buddha's labor.

. . . . .

From the very beginning a difference was made between the spirit and the letter. The Teacher said, "Knowledge is not the letter, but the spirit."

The word of Buddha is different from the letter. The Teacher communicates the Truth to the disciple, but only after deep and personal realization can the pupil possess it.

According to the words of Buddhist scholars the premise upon which the Teaching is based answers all demands of reason, but to confound reason with the limited mind of ignorant man would be exceedingly absurd.

To this day there are preserved a sufficient number of Buddhist legends, more or less authentic, to permit us at least approximately to know the character of the Teacher's discourses. From these traditions we know that the Teacher never hesitated to answer questions put to him. In the ancient compilations of Buddha's words an unusual conciseness and definiteness of expressions is evident above all. The *Sutras* are nothing but the aphorisms or concise sayings of Buddha, containing the philosophical and moral statutes of the Teaching. The aphorisms of Buddha retained their conciseness in Buddhist traditions, but already with the addition of comments.

The vividness of the Teaching of Buddha was contained also in the power of his simple expressions. Never did he apply any verses. Verily, like a lion, he roared about the purity of life. Never did he preach, but only explained on occasion, using parables to emphasize the given advice.

Buddha ordained that his disciples should always expound the Teaching in the colloquial language and severely censured each attempt to codify the Teaching in an artificial literary language. In Buddhist traditions indications exist about the travels of the Teacher beyond the contemporaneous boundaries of India, into Tibet, Khotan and Altai.

THE TRADITIONS OF BUDDHISM—to have in its communities large schools with courses in philosophy, medicine, mathematics, astronomy, and other subjects —are the direct result of the covenants of the Teacher, who pointed out that "ignorance is a stain, which stains man beyond all other things."

The Buddhist schools, as well as the exact contents of their literary treasures, are little known to outsiders, but each new point of information serves to broaden Western understanding about the inner structure of Buddhism. Without language, without knowledge, without faith, no one can penetrate into those strongholds to which the community, the *Sangha*, is so near.

Let us not forget that the word *lama* means teacher, and not monk as is often understood through ignorance. Since ancient times learned lamas copied and printed books from engraved plates and were highly skilled artists, with complete anonymity in authorship. Reverence for books and libraries is traditional in Tibet. Among learned lamas a custom exists to lock him who is defeated in an intellectual debate into a library.

The restoration of the ancient *Vinaya*, the Rules of moral and communal precepts of Buddhism, has always, and especially now, stood as the immediate task of Buddhist communal gatherings.

A Russian scholar, in a lecture delivered by him in Petrograd at an exhibition of Buddhist objects, said, "We must say that the foundations of the Buddhist philosophical teaching, correctly understood and translated into our philosophical language, reveal an extraordinary affinity with precisely the latest, the newest achievements in the domain of our scientific conception of the world. 'Universe without God,' 'psychology without an unchanging soul,' 'the eternity of the elements of matter and spirit' which is only a special manifestation of the law of causality; heredity, a vital process instead of the existence of things; and in the domain of practical life the denial of the rights of personal possession, the denial of national limitation, the universal brotherhood of all peoples, without the rights of private property; finally, the general, and for us all, indispensable inevitable faith that we move and must move toward perfection, regardless of soul and free will—these are the fundamental traits of the Buddhist, as well as of our contemporary new conception of the world." Precisely the Teaching of Buddha refutes the existing fallacy that evolution is stable and its laws act irrespectively. We know that everything lives and moves individually, thus there must be a special coordination and discipline in order that balance, or harmony, not be impaired. To say that man must evolute in spite of himself as part of the general plan of evolution would mean to make man no better than a playball of destiny.

One must point out with regret that the last words of this distinguished lecturer, "we are moving and must move toward perfection, *regardless of free will*," are in evident contradiction to the fundamental principle of the Teaching, which, for the possibility of perfection and achievement of the highest conscious existence, demands absolutely personal efforts and assiduous self-exertion.

L ET US CONSIDER Buddhism and contemporary science. It is evident that Buddhists are most open to all
evolutionary achievements. Of course, this quality was
instilled by their basic Teaching. Becoming familiar with
the foundations we see how greatly the statements of
the Teacher are confirmed by the achievements of our
contemporary science. The same results which Einstein
reached by way of experiment were reached by ancient
Buddhists in a purely contemplative way.

Once more, we repeat that Buddhism cannot be
regarded as a religious revelation, because Gotama
Buddha affirmed his Teaching as the apprehension of
eternal truths, which were likewise propounded by his
predecessors.

Gotama taught that all that exists issued from Akasha,
or primary substance, in conformation with the law of
motion inherent in it and dissolves after a certain period
of existence.

"Nothing comes from nothing." Buddhists do not
believe in miracles; consequently they deny the Creation
and cannot conceive of the creation of something from
nothing. "Nothing organic is eternal. Everything is in a
state of continuous flux, undergoing change, and sus-
taining the continuity according to the law of evolution."

"The world exists by cause. All things exist by cause.
All beings are bound by cause."[4]

Regarding the constant change of the world, visible
to our coarse organs, as well as it dissolution, Buddhism
points out that those dissolutions are temporary and

periodical; for, according to the principle of evolution guided by the law of individual and collective Karma, the disappearing world will in turn manifest a new world with all its contents, just as our Universe was manifested from the primary substance—matter.

Denying miracles, the Teacher pointed out the concealed powers of human nature which, when developed, can produce the so-called miracles.

The method of developing these powers is interpreted in Buddhist books and is known under the name of the science "Iddhi-Vidhanana," which points out two forms of manifestation of these powers and two ways to attain them. One, the lower, is reached by way of various ascetic and other physical practices; the other higher one, embracing all possible manifestations, is attained by the power of inner development.

The first method of developing these powers is not lasting and may be lost, whereas inner development can never be lost. Its mastery is attained by following the noble way indicated by Buddha.

All these hidden powers gradually unfold in man, usually of themselves, in proportion to man's mastery of the lower expressions of his nature in a whole series of previous lives.

For the development of powers of the higher grade, four conditions are indispensable:

1. Will;
2. Its exertion;
3. Mental development;
4. The discrimination between truth and error.

A man possessing these powers or knowledge, increasing nature's powers, can perform the most unusual miracles; in other words, he can execute any scientific experiment. Buddha did not encourage manifestations of powers, which lead only to confusion in minds ignorant of the principles that are represented by those manifestations and which create a heavy atmosphere of forcibly disturbed elements.

The *Mahapari-Nirvana Sutra* tells about an unusual light emanating from the body of Buddha which was observed by his nearest disciple Ananda. The Teacher pointed out that on two occasions such physical radiation could become visible to the physical eye:

1. At the time of the great enlightenment of a man who becomes Buddha;

2. On the night when such a man—Buddha—finally departed.

Studying the Buddhist sources one finds many valuable indications about the purely physical manifestation of radiation. It is indicated as of a luminous and most subtle quality which surrounds man and is the nearest inner agent of human perception. "This matter is exceedingly fine, like the radiance of a diamond, imponderable, incombustible, disappearing after death without any traces. Nevertheless it is atomic."

Nowadays this radiation is known to Europeans under the name of *aura*. This radiation is quite normal and it has been scientifically proved that not only all human and animal organisms possess it, but even trees, plants, and stones.

The first of the scholars and scientists to point out this characteristic was Baron Reichenbach. He proved this radiation to be quite natural and his experiments were expounded in detail in his *Researches of 1844–45*.

Similarly in Paris, Dr. Baraduc took photographs of this radiation, and now in London, America, and Berlin whole institutions are devoted to the study of human emanations—auras. It has been proved that this radiation may be of different shades, that it expands in volume, and grows in intensity of light, according to the spiritual and intellectual development of the man. Such manifestations as sudden flashes of colored rays emanating from the shoulders have also been noted. But science has not found any explanation for the origin of such flashes. Mention has been made of the decrease in power of the light of these emanations during ailing conditions of the organism.

In her book, *The Magnetic Aura of the Cosmic Man,* Mar-Galittu (Mrs. J. P. Reimann) writes: "Professor Yourevitch of Moscow points out the Y-rays of the human aura, as a newly discovered, highly powerful and invisible radiation.

"After a decade of detailed experiment, Professor Yourevitch brought the results of his investigations before the International Psychological Congress, which took place last year at Copenhagen.

"The difference between the human emanations and those of radium and the Roentgen rays is that human emanations are far subtler and can penetrate dense walls, whereas the Roentgen rays and radium depend upon a definite density of the bodies which they penetrate. The emanations, for instance, transform gaseous streams, otherwise non-conductors, into remarkable conductors of magnetic force. Their far-reaching conductivity is the chief basic quality of the Y-rays. Without respect for distance and intensity, these gaseous streams become conductive under the influence of human emanations. Their far-reaching and penetrative power is conditioned by the cosmic contact of human emanations and therefore they are conceded to have a stronger effect than all other rays.

"Beyond their capacity for far-reaching conductivity and power of penetration, the Y-rays have the power, when piercing thick obstructions, to exercise mechanical functions as well. When piercing thick metal plates, the Y-rays cause molecular sediments as soon as the rays pass through in a consciously concentrated way. During certain experiments they induce refraction of light-waves. They may also be photographed. The Y-rays of the aura are at the basis of levitation and telekinetic phenomena. The work of Professor Yourevitch, which is called 'Y-rays as Conductors of Biophysical Energy' contains fifty photographs of his experiments."

The contemporary theory of hypnotic suggestion may be found in the following legend about Chullapanthaka in the Pali commentaries on the Dhammapada:

"Chullapanthaka was a disciple who had mastered some of the powers. One day Buddha sent for him, and when the messenger reached the Sangha, he saw three hundred disciples sitting in a group, each of them an exact image of the other. To his question, 'Which is Chullapanthaka?' every one of the three hundred answered, 'I am Chullapanthaka.' The messenger returned to his Teacher disconcerted, but Buddha ordered him to return immediately and if the same thing should occur, to take the first one who called himself Chullapanthaka by the hand and bring him to Buddha." The Teacher knew that the disciple desired to display his newly acquired power by suggesting to the consciousness of the messenger his illusive image. This power is called "Mahamaya Iddhi" and in order to manifest it, Chullapanthaka had vividly to represent in his mind his own image and then to suggest it up to the desired number to the consciousness of the messenger.

In the same way, contemporary scientific data support the theory of karma expounded in Buddhism. Contemporary science teaches that each generation of man is heir to the distinctive characteristics of preceding generations, not only in mass but in each individual case.

Psychology finds its raison d'etre in that exclusive and strong attention which Buddha apportions to the mental processes, to the purification and expansion of the consciousness of his disciples by affirming thought as the dominant factor in the evolution of all that exists. The psychological processes in Buddhism are closely connected with physiology.

Buddhism does not trace any line of demarcation between psychic processes and matter. The psychic processes are regarded as the manifestations of the subtlest qualities of matter.

In the *Dialogues of the Buddha*, Part II, we find an indication about the existence in addition to a physical body of a mental body which is its exact counterpart and which can be externalized at will and become active at great distances.

"With his mind thus concentrated, completely purified, utterly clear, devoid of depravity, free of taint, ready to act, firm and imperturbable, he applies and directs it to evoking the mental body. He calls up from this body another body, having form, made of thought-stuff, having all limbs and parts, not lacking any organ. It is as if a man were to pull out a reed from its sheath. He would know: 'This is the reed, this the sheath. The reed is one thing, the sheath another. It is from the sheath that the reed has been drawn forth. Just so, the bhikshu calls up from this body another body, having form, made of thought-stuff, having all limbs and parts, not lacking any organ." [28]

Asserting the indestructibility of energy, Buddha regarded all that exists as aggregates of the finest energies.

For the physicist of today the moving power is matter, man's perception of matter being the response of his senses to the vibrations of energy.

And what is Dharma, if not energy?

Dharmas, according to Buddhism, exist for us by their effects; all our perceptions being, above all, dharmas.

Therefore, translating this formula into contemporary language, we may say that all sense-perceptions are exclusively energy effects and energy is the only real existing entity.

Similarly, his affirmations about thought acting at a distance antedate our researches in the domain of thought-transmission and wireless. Since thought is energy then, as such, it is subject to the same law in its action as any other energy. We know that the hertzian waves are emitted for a thousand miles into space without any wires, with the result that they can be caught by any equally attuned receiver. Why, then, cannot man send out a thought-energy which will evoke identical vibrations in the man susceptible to them?

Thus, Buddha is our predecessor in many domains of knowledge.

Buddha also pointed out the difference that exists between the evident and the reality. His comparison of the evident to a mirage or illusion (Maya) is applicable to any contemporary discussion.

This Great Wisdom, if studied not in the letter but in its spirit, would enrich an unprejudiced mind with many a priceless gem.

The philosophy of Buddhism may be termed the analysis of separate elements attracted into combination by the formation of a definite individual stream. The individual stream is accumulated and fed by numberless manifestations of man on Earth, on other planes and other worlds. Absorbing all the characteristics of each manifestation, this stream swells in possibilities, transforming and remaining eternally self-containing. True individuality, true immortality, is contained in the realization of the true "I" which is constructed by innumerable combinations of human manifestations.

"All concern about the personality is in vain; the self is like a mirage, all tribulations that touch it will pass away. They will vanish like a nightmare when the sleeper awakens."

In Buddhism man is not a futile pygmy as he appears to Western mind, but the lord of the worlds. Being part of the Cosmos, like it, he is limitless in his possibilities.

The data about cosmic creation, about the existence of innumerable world systems in eternal motion, which are manifested and dissolved; the affirmations of the inhabitance of the multitude of worlds and about the full coordination of organisms which populate these worlds with the properties and structure of their planet, coincide with those scientific problems which at present agitate the minds of the true scientists.

Thus, contemporary science, in accord with the affirmation of fundamental Buddhism, confirms the very realistic essence of this Teaching of the reality of the life-creative essence of great Matter, impressed for the first time.

Let us pay due homage to that Great Mind which, impelled by a powerful Spirit, fathomed the very foundations of Existence, solved the problems of life and pointed out the goals of evolution as conscious cooperation with the Cosmos and communion with the far-off worlds.

NO TEACHING FORESAW the future with such precision as Buddhism. Parallel with reverence for Buddha, Buddhism develops the veneration of Bodhisattvas—future Buddhas. According to the tradition, Gotama, before reaching the state of Buddha, had been a Bodhisattva for many centuries. The word Bodhisattva comprises two concepts: Bodhi—enlightenment or awakening, and Sattva—the essence. Who are these Bodhisattvas? The disciples of Buddhas, who voluntarily have renounced their personal liberation and, following the example of their Teachers, have entered upon a long, weary, thorny path of help to humanity. Such Bodhisattvas appear on Earth in the midst of the most varying conditions of life. Physically indistinguishable in any way from the rest of humanity, they differ completely in their psychology, constantly being the heralds of the principle of the common welfare.

Buddha, directing all possibilities toward the affirmation of evolution, bade his disciples venerate the future Buddhas more than the Buddhas of the past. "Thus as the new moon is worshipped more than the full moon, so those who have faith in Me must reverence Bodhisattvas more than Buddhas." [26]

History has not revealed to us elsewhere such a living example of self-denial. According to tradition, the Blessed One preordained the Bodhisattva Maitreya as his successor.

"And the Blessed One said to Ananda, 'I am not the first Buddha who has come upon Earth, nor shall I be the last. In due time another Buddha will arise in the world, a Holy One, a supremely enlightened One, endowed with wisdom in conduct, embracing the Universe, an incomparable leader of men, a ruler of devas and mortals. He will reveal to you the same eternal truths, that I have taught you. He will establish his Law, glorious in its origin, glorious at the climax, and glorious at the goal, in the spirit and in the letter. He will proclaim a righteous life, wholly perfect and pure, such as I now proclaim. His disciples will number many thousands while mine number many hundreds.'

"Ananda said, 'How shall we know him?'

"The Blessed One said, 'He will be known as Maitreya!' " [13]

The future Buddha, Maitreya, as his name indicates, is the Buddha of compassion and love. This Bodhisattva, according to the power of his qualities, is often called Ajita—the Invincible.

It is interesting to note that reverence of many Bodhisattvas was accepted and developed only in the Mahayana school. Nevertheless, the reverence of one Bodhisattva, Maitreya, as a successor chosen by Buddha himself, is accepted also in the Hinayana. Thus, one Bodhisattva, Maitreya, embraces the complete scope, being the personification of all aspirations of Buddhism.

What qualities must a Bodhisattva possess? In the Teaching of Gotama Buddha and in the Teaching of Bodhisattva Maitreya, given by him to Asanga according to tradition in the fourth century (*Mahayana-Sutralankara*), the maximum development of energy, courage, patience, constancy of striving, and fearlessness was underlined first of all. Energy is the basis of everything, for it alone contains all possibilities.

"Buddhas are eternally in action; immovability is unknown to them; like the eternal motion in space the actions of the Sons of Conquerors manifest themselves in the worlds."

"Mighty, valiant, firm in his step, not rejecting the burden of an achievement for the General Good."

"There are three joys of Bodhisattvas; the joy of giving, the joy of helping, and the joy of eternal perception. Patience always, in all, and everywhere. The Sons of Buddhas, the Sons of Conquerors, Bodhisattvas in their active compassion are Mothers to All-Existence."[27]

Throughout the entire Buddhist world the rocks on the roadsides, with the images of Maitreya, point out the approaching future. From the most ancient times until now this Image has been erected by Buddhists who know the approach of the New Era. In our day, venerable lamas, accompanied by disciples, painters, and sculptors, travel through the Buddhist countries, erecting new images of the symbol of aspirations toward the radiant future.

· · · · ·

The Teaching of Buddha must be verified and should be given for broad knowledge. In our time, it is strange to think about the community and not to know the foundations of the first Scientist-Exponent of the community. The hand of Buddha was tireless in preparing the experiment of the world's laboratory.

The fact that Buddha ordained the World Community as the evolution of humanity, in itself gives to his Teaching its fiery persuasion.

In Buddha's structure one may move through endless stories, and the doors everywhere will be open to the call of the community. The exact knowledge of Buddha permitted him to determine the exact condition of his contemporaries and to perceive the universal community only in the far-off future.

Respect for Buddha was such that no one obscured the image of the Teacher with the garb of divinity. Buddha is impressed on minds as a Man, a Teacher who affirms. In this leonine fiery affirmation he attained a prevision of Maitreya—the symbol of the era of comprehension of the greatness of matter and affirmation of the great universal community!

. . . . .

Said the Blessed One, "Distinguish between those who understand and those who agree. He who understands the Teaching will not tarry in applying it to life, he who agrees will nod and extol the Teaching as remarkable wisdom, but will not apply this wisdom to life.

"There are many who have agreed, but they are like a withered forest, fruitless and without shade. Only decay awaits them.

"Those who understand are few, but like a sponge they absorb the precious knowledge and are ready to cleanse the horrors of the world with the precious liquid.

"He who has understood cannot help applying the Teaching, because realizing goal-fitness he accepts it as a solution of life.

"Do not waste much time with the agreeing ones. Let them first demonstrate the application of the first call."

Thus is attributed to the Blessed One the goal-fitting attitude to newcomers.

. . . . .

All this means that the purification of the Teaching will rest not only on the acceptance of its foundations, but on its application in life. An abstract understanding of the Teaching of the Blessed One is impossible. We see how greatly it penetrates into life when we realize how entire countries fell away from the Teaching, when instead of applying it to life they turned it into abstract discourses. In Tibet a lessening of the religious interest is apparent. One can even notice the increase of the Bon Teaching, the antithesis of Buddhism.

The Tashi Lama found it impossible to remain in Tibet. Following his example many of the best lamas have left Tibet. Without these educated lamas, the religious life of Tibet has become dormant.

Such examples are useful in observing how the distortion of the Teaching is effected.

At the same time one can see what victory the Teaching carries into other countries where people are concerned with applying the foundations in life.

The same task is accomplished by the new tendency toward toleration of the followers of Hinayana.

Buddha, as the source, and Maitreya, as a universal hope, will unite the austere followers of the Teaching of the South with the multiformity of the North.

That which is most essential for the immediate future will definitely manifest itself. Instead of swelling the Teaching with commentaries, it will again be restored to the beauty of the value of concise conviction. The new time of the Era of Maitreya is in need of conviction. Life in its entirety must be purified by the flame of achievement. The great Buddha, who preordained Maitreya, prescribed the path for the whole of existence. For those wise and clear covenants, the manifestation of the new evolution is calling.

The demand for the purification of the Teaching is not accidental. The dates are approaching. The Image of Maitreya is ready to rise. All the Buddhas of the past have combined their wisdom of experience and have handed it on to the Blessed Coming One.

. . . . .

The lama proclaims, "Let life be firm as adamant; victorious as the banner of the Teacher; mighty as an eagle, and may it last for eternity."

SOURCES

1. *Anguttara-Nikaya.*
2. Ashvaghosha, *Fo-Sho-Hing-Tsun-King, A Life of Buddha*, the Chinese version of *Buddhacarita*.
3. Buddhist Birth Stories, or *Jataka Tales*.
4. *Majjhima-Nikaya.*
5. *Sikshasamuccaya*, compiled by Santideva.
6. Santideva, *Bodhicaryavatara*.
7. *Sutta-Nipata.*
8. *Dhammapada.*
9. *Mahavagga.*
10. M. P. Grimblot, *Sept Suttas Palis*.
11. *The Jataka.*
12. *Milinda-Panha, The Questions of King Milinda*.
13. Paul Carus, *The Gospel of Buddha*.
14. *Samyutta-Nikaya.*
15. *Itivuttaka.*
16. *Sutra of Forty-two Sections*.
17. *The Udana.*
18. Ashvaghosha, *Buddhacarita*.
19. *Mahapari-Nirvana Sutra, The Book of the Great Decease*.
20. *Katha-Vatthu.*
21. *Mahavastu.*
22. *Saddharma-Pundarika, The Lotus of the Wonderful Law*.
23. *Madhyamakavritti.*
24. *Lalitavistara.*
25. Soyen-Shaku, *Sermons of a Buddhist*.
26. *Madyamakavatara*
27. *Mahayana-Sutralankara.*
28. *Digha-Nikaya.*
29. *Vinaya Culavagga.*

CPSIA information can be obtained
at www.ICGtesting.com
Printed in the USA
FFHW012320130219
50522254-55785FF

9 781946 742360